DISCARD

EUROPE OVERSEAS

RAYMOND F. BETTS, Professor of History at Grinnell College, Iowa, is the author of *The "Scramble" for Africa* and *Assimilation and Association in French Colonial Theory*.

Raymond F. Betts

EUROPE OVERSEAS:

PHASES *of* IMPERIALISM

Basic Books, Inc., Publishers

NEW YORK / LONDON

© 1968 by Basic Books, Inc.
Library of Congress Catalog Card Number: 68–19772
Manufactured in the United States of America
Designed by Kay Eaglin

To Kenny and Jimmy

PREFACE

This is a small volume on a large subject. The reader therefore might be led immediately to the conclusion that it is either modest or presumptuous. As the author, I hope that it is the former. No single volume, whatever its proportions, can easily bring between its covers the many aspects and problems of imperialism. The global scope of modern empire still beggars the imagination and perplexes the thoughtful mind. Moreover, our own chronological proximity to this historical phenomenon may still deny us that proper perspective from which a general and complete view can be obtained.

Any student of modern overseas expansion knows the

excitement derived from its study, and he also knows the effort involved in obtaining a balanced judgment of its history. The notion of empire is often preceded by a glittering array of adjectives and is equally often followed by a dismal train of invective. It is seldom approached indifferently. Worse and better fates have befallen man, of course, but few have been more significant, more grandiose in conception, more striking in execution, more commented on in retrospect.

This book is designed to be an introduction to the subject. It in no manner pretends to recapitulate the history of European overseas expansion. What it does attempt to do is to present the major phases in that expansion. With this purpose in mind I have not freighted the study with volumes of detailed facts. Yet I trust that I have not treated these facts frivolously. The study has been supported by them, but it tends to ride above them. Where a salient quotation or a provocative argument has been presented, or where a source is rather obscure, I have provided the necessary reference so that the interested reader can investigate further. Otherwise the pages are not heavily encumbered with references.

Any study of imperialism presents a problem of vocabulary: how to avoid words with pejorative connotations. Terms used by European proponents of empire now seem archaic, condescending, or smug. I have tried to avoid such terms wherever possible, but I do admit to using one frequently, and this because it is an omnibus word whose descriptive qualities are not easily matched. When I employ "native" I do so to refer to the resident population of a region already installed before the European presence was made known, nothing more.

Like most general studies, this one derives from many sources and many minds. I lay no claim to great originality, and I am certain that arguments and propositions herein presented may have already appeared here, there, or elsewhere without my knowledge of them. There is some comfort, however, in knowing, even if belatedly, that other people think along lines similar to your own—or vice versa.

I take no little satisfaction in the knowledge that most of this study was written in Dakar, now capital of the Republic of Senegal. That former French city, today a nexus of the new Africa, stands as an enduring monument to the conception of some aspects of modern empire. To me, however, that city is an agglomeration of Senegalese of many tribal origins who have displayed a friendliness and a courtesy to a Westerner—who is in addition white—that suggest modern imperialism did not everywhere leave behind effects that were acutely bitter or eternally marring.

Again I extend my thanks to my wife Jackie, who has read and typed the manuscript without complaint and with good humor. And I must also thank my children—Kenny, Jimmy, and Susan—who have tried to understand.

Raymond F. Betts

January 1968

CONTENTS

EUROPE OVERSEAS

1 . OVER THE SEAS
AND FAR AWAY

An American senator of some half-century ago suggested
that the general enthusiasm for imperialism was the result of "earth hunger." His metaphor was not inappropriate, for the appetite of most peoples and nations over
the centuries for more land, for ever-expanding frontiers
as sources of economic gain—and perhaps, on occasion,
of greater personal freedom—has been sharp. Just as
the Romans embraced the Mediterranean Sea, as the
Germans of the late Middle Ages pushed eastward into
the marshlands, and as Americans spilled over the Appa-
lachians and Russians over the Urals, so did Europeans
leave their shores to carry their ideas, goods, and power

abroad. The similarities among all of these enterprises are both obvious and striking; moreover, they suggest that the restlessness of man—the search after adventure, wealth, new surroundings—may be a basic ingredient of human nature.

While most studies of imperialism have been ocean-bound, with little attention directed toward land frontiers, this tendency has been criticized of late and has been considered the result of a "salt-water fallacy," a false distinction between transoceanic and transcontinental empires. The criticism certainly has its appeal. Who, indeed, is to say that there is a sharp division between the activities of the British colonial army which laid siege to Fort Duquesne and the activities of the American army which fought against Mexico nearly a century later? Or were the *coureurs du bois* who played such a significant role in the French fur-trading empire in Canada any different in attitude and purpose from the *promyshlenniks* who were equally significant in the Russian Siberian fur trade? Moreover, was the Russian absorption of Georgia in the nineteenth century any different in intent from the British absorption of Burma in the same century? Such questions do yield answers which seem to confirm the existence of a salt-water fallacy. With these thoughts in mind, one could simply define imperialism as the propensity to forceful expansion. Such a definition would allow for extended historical limits, probably beginning with that long removed moment imagined by Rousseau when one man divided off a piece of land and said, "This is mine." Or, put in more political terms, imperialism might be defined as the foreign policy of a state or a people directed toward the acquisition of more power. Napoleon, Teddy Roosevelt, Hitler, and Stalin were all imperialists, as were Cecil Rhodes, Hubert Lyautey, Carl Peters, and Admiral Mahan—each trying to enhance his country's power by extending its geographical boundaries.

Initially, then, the student of imperialism is confronted with the perplexing problem of finding a meaningful definition. If imperialism is considered in terms of earth hunger and power politics, does not the term include most of the foreign affairs of states and nations throughout recorded history? Where does one begin and end the study? Is there not, ironically, an academic imperialism of imperialism?

Like "war" and "revolution," "imperialism" is generally understood, even if it is not defined. It is a generic term that is very familiar to most of us living today. Like war and revolution, imperialism is both a political and a social process, one which leads to the alteration of the disposition of power and of the control of society. But beyond this it parts company with these other historical phenomena.

As a working definition the following is proposed: imperialism is that consciously undertaken state activity in which force, intrigue, or even negotiation is employed to secure the long-range political or economic domination by the state of foreign territory or foreign peoples it wishes for some reason to control. The definition must remain general, but it does suggest certain limits. Imperialism should not be simply equated with war, nor should it be confused with the sudden incursion, or *raz-*

zia, which does not lead to permanent occupation. More-over, it should not be considered purposeless, a sort of unconscious movement outward. Underlying motives may be mixed, even confused, but whatever these motives and subsequent analyses of them are, the imperialist sponsor—individual, group, or class—is aware of and committed to its activities, which it invariably undertakes in the name of the state. This point is important. Either the state comes to assume responsibility for the expansionist act, whatever its immediate cause, or it disavows that act, in which case there is no real instance of imperialism, only some private or group intrigue on the international level. It is generally agreed, therefore, that imperialism is a significant aspect of foreign policy. While principally a European phenomenon of the last four centuries, imperialism is not exclusively such, for it is neither territorially nor culturally restricted.

The history of imperialism, like all history, is no doubt of one piece, but it can be cut into meaningful segments according to time and place. Expansion has always been severely conditioned by the geographical, economic, and social milieus in which it takes place, and particular imperialist policies will therefore vary accordingly. Thus, for instance, the differences between early Assyrian expansion and that of the French Third Republic, two millennia later, are as clear and as meaningful as their similarities. To return to an earlier argument, if transoceanic and transcontinental imperialisms are comparable, they are also different. Contiguity and noncontiguity may not always be the decisive factors, but they are never without significance.

To emphasize this distinction more forcefully, the neologism "colonialism" has been recently employed.[1] Although the term, like imperialism, soon became shrouded in polemics, it basically means that form of imperialism which takes place overseas and in which a dominating society, basing its rule on superior force, exploits the indigenous population and the land now under its control. In particular, the term has been used to describe the most recent phase of overseas imperialism, that of the late nineteenth century, and the countries which have usually been labeled colonialist are Great Britain, France, Belgium, and Holland. The French, in their own effort to provide clarity where ambiguity seems to reside, have hit upon a combination of terms, *l'impérialisme colonial*, to identify modern overseas imperialism.

Without pursuing these semantic differences any further, we can perhaps best single out the distinctions by providing the following rule of thumb: the closer the dominated territory to the dominating power, the greater the opportunity for political relatedness. Contiguous imperialism usually results in political absorption; it is like a spot of oil in which the stain extends more or less evenly. Where successful, as in the United States and Russia, a political system of marked integration came into existence. Where aborted, as in Napoleon's Grand Empire or Hitler's Third Reich, absorption was at least partial, if only temporary. Parts of Italy and the Rhine-

---

[1] The term has a rather old origin. For instance, the French Socialist Paul Louis used it in this sense in his short study, *Le Colonialisme* (Paris, 1905).

land were joined with France, as Austria and the Sudetenland were incorporated into Germany. Very few are the examples of noncontiguous imperialism leading to successful political absorption: most recently Hawaii and Alaska stand out in the American instance; Guadaloupe and Martinique, in the French. For the most part, professions of political absorption and equal treatment, as those made by France with respect to Algeria, or Portugal with respect to Mozambique and Angola, bear little relationship to stark realities.

Noncontiguous imperialism seldom results in political absorption. Regardless of its supporting theory, each colonial system has exhibited a considerable degree of political autonomy. While the British theoretically moved in this direction, even the French, with their elegant doctrine of political and cultural assimilation, varied their rule according to clime and terrain and never seriously applied their favorite doctrine to the alien peoples they ruled. This state of affairs was everywhere first conditioned by an obvious geographical factor: the expanse of ocean which divided colony from metropole. As a result, the colonial territory was often removed from strict or direct central governmental control in the pre-air age and thus of necessity allowed some degree of local political development. More important, the distance usually meant a distinct difference between the imperialist nation and its institutions and the imperialized region and its institutions. Usually the distance could not be bridged. Political development remained peculiar to the area in which it took place, so that commonality of cultural interests, no matter how ardently stressed, was seldom strong enough to counter this development or compensate for it. Even in one of the earlier and more hardy attempts at cultural assimilation—Spain in the Philippines—the policy did not lead to auspicious or permanent results. And in the most obvious and praised examples of transoceanic imperialism—the British dominions—the tendency over the years has been away from the mother country, so that today the Commonwealth of Nations is a pleasant name, a noble idea, but far from being a strong political force.

Granted that both land and sea empires have been created by the amalgamation of large blocks of territory—the historian Theodore Mommsen once wrote that the "history of every nation, and especially the Latin nation, is a vast system of amalgamations"—the former usually leads to fusion, the latter to disintegration. The motto of the successful land empire might well be that of the United States, *E Pluribus Unum*, but no sea empire could use this device. Without exception this latter form of empire seems to follow the reverse process by which it was built up. The "blocks" that were acquired and amalgamated now fall away, one by one. Ortega y Gasset saw the Spanish Empire so disintegrate,[2] and one need only observe the collapse of the French Empire for recent confirmation: first Indochina fell away, then most of North Africa, finally West and Equatorial Africa.

[2] See the essay "Invertebrate Spain" in his collection of essays translated and published under the title *Invertebrate Spain* (London, 1937).

If reduced to physical terms of motion, contiguous expansion becomes centripetal; noncontiguous becomes centrifugal.

It must be admitted, however, that if the direction of motion and the results of that motion are different, the character of contiguous and noncontiguous expansion may have been similar on occasion. For instance, Russian and American continental expansion in the nineteenth century bears a strong resemblance to the British and Spanish settlement empires of the sixteenth and seventeenth centuries. Colonists moved into marginal lands, either mingling with, displacing, or exterminating the indigenous population, and bringing with them the intellectual and political baggage they carried from back East or West, whichever the point of departure. In the strictest sense these were colonial developments, the migrations of peoples to lands recently opened to settlement. It should not be surprising, then, to find some authors comparing American colonial and continental experience in terms of expanding frontiers.[3]

Later overseas expansion diverges sharply from this particular pattern. If anything, it has a certain resemblance to that of the early trade empires established by the Portuguese and Dutch in Asia. No settlement colonies, no great migrations from one point to another characterize this imperialism. In the new empires carved out by the European nations—and the United States and Japan, for that matter—the term "colonial" takes on a different meaning. It means possession, a territory apper-

[3] See Walter Prescott Webb, *The Great Frontier* (Boston, 1952), particularly p. 13.

taining to a metropolitan nation, but not a place to which emigrants stream and take root; it is, in short, not a part of the national body politic. Large indigenous populations, insalubrious climates, and still easy access to the New World all militated against the establishment of large numbers of European settlers abroad in the new empires. The possessions comprising these empires were, in the word of one French colonial writer, "dominations," areas dominated by, not peopled by, Europeans.[4]

What developed in each such area was a pluralistic society of sorts, with the European everywhere a demographic minority but everywhere the significant political and cultural force. Unlike American and Russian continental expansion, there was no repulsion or no assimilation of the local populations. The European remained, with the possible exception of South Africa, an outsider; and, with no exception, preferred living in a world of his own rather than mingle with and join the indigenous population and its society. The much discussed "colour bar" in Subsaharan Africa is the most obvious example of the results of this attitude. Cultures in contact, cultures in collision; such is the basic nature of the problem of modern overseas empire.

Turning to the aspect of imperialism with which this study will be most particularly concerned, that of the late nineteenth and early twentieth centuries, one can argue that its distinctiveness derives from its noncontiguous, nonsettlement character. Perhaps these two negative as-

[4] The argument is worth pursuing. See Jules Harmand, *Domination et colonisation* (Paris, 1910).

pects suggest that this imperialism was bound to be ephemeral, that nothing positive enough was ever developed to withstand the strong tug of mid-twentieth-century nationalism in the Third World.

These new empires were administrative and expropriative empires.

1) *European residence was minimal or temporary.* Few settlers moved permanently into the new Asian portions of European empire, and those who went to Africa, with the exception of South Africa and Algeria, were small in number. Much of the South African population grew from pre-existing white stock, and of the one million Europeans living in Algeria at the time of independence, only half were French. Some 200,000 whites now dominate Rhodesia, but elsewhere population statistics are less significant. All territories considered, the permanent European resident population was but a demographic drop in the human bucket. As for the administrators who provided the skeleton of European empire, residence was of course temporary, and a sense of detachment from the indigenous populations being administered was a common attitude. In the 1920's and 1930's the quality and interest of the administrators in the lower echelons improved, and an attempt to appreciate and evaluate indigenous societies was genuinely made. Even then, the administrator remained a temporary resident and only most infrequently felt that he belonged to the land.

2) *The lands were not worked by European labor, but by native hands.* The economic development of the colonial territories may have been a European charge, but it was realized by native labor. With the exception of a few choice areas, such as the highlands in Kenya, the European found no great opportunity for comfortable or permanent agricultural or ranching activity. His chief economic activities centered on the extractive industries—Moroccan phosphates, South African gold—or trade and commerce. Generally he sought to make a "competence" and then to return home, much in the manner of the eighteenth-century "nabob," but seldom with such rewarding results. Thus, like the administrator, he was temporarily attached to the land. It was the native who did most of the work: sometimes on a colonial plantation, sometimes on his own in order to pay European-imposed taxes, sometimes under force, and sometimes in the Eurasian or Eurafrican city in order to earn a wage.

3) *The social components were never fused.* As has already been said, the Europeans remained detached from native society. The "system of Saint Moritz" was the way one French writer described Anglo-India, with the British living on the high ground, the Hindus below. This lack of social integration often led to conflicting cultural and political interests. According to Nehru in *Discovery of India*, the European attitude impaired cultural growth.

Alien rule is inevitably cut off from the creative energies of the people it dominates. When this alien rule has its own economic and cultural center far from the subject country and is further backed by racialism, this divorce is complete, and leads to spiritual and cultural starvation of the subject peoples.

The English scholar John Plamenatz holds a somewhat contrary view. His convincing argument states that the very lack of social integration was an effective element in modernization. Remaining apart from and alien to the peoples they controlled—and Plamenatz has India particularly in mind—the Europeans drew these peoples to them, not vice versa, and hence suggested a new way of life.[5]

4) *Indigenous political systems were not always abolished, nor were they ever successfully reformed.* The Europeans did often honestly direct native policy; however, they did this with a detachment which at once suggested efficiency and justice, but also suggested little genuine interest in local political development. Administration was the key word, not politics. Bureaucratic empires, not political systems, arose. The Europeans ruled from above, and, with a certain *noblesse oblige*, fulfilled their self-prescribed responsibilities. The staffing of these autocratic, bureaucratic empires was done primarily by Europeans. As late as 1951, for instance, of three

[5] John Plamenatz, *On Alien Rule and Self-Government* (London, 1960), p. 14.

thousand senior civil servants in Nigeria, only seven hundred were Nigerians. While the Europeans did much for the native populations, they allowed next to nothing to be done by them.

5) *Indigenous populations remained mostly untrained and illiterate.* While the European imperialists had noble intentions about their civilizing missions, they seldom had the capital or the personnel to introduce effective popular educational systems. Moreover, they assumed that such an educational task would be a long haul and hasty action should therefore be avoided. One French critic argued that it would be ten thousand years before the African would be like the Frenchman—as if this were necessarily the measure of political and social maturity! Colonial educational policy might be described in the pitiful words: too late and too little. In that *pays d'élection* of modern European imperialism, Africa, the illiteracy rate was still between 80 per cent and 85 per cent among people fifteen years old and over, according to a UNESCO survey of 1958.

To the Europeans initially observing the new empires they had acquired, the task ahead was a clear one. The administrators assumed that their chief responsibilities were to maintain order and also to make empire pay, or, at the very least, to assure that it did not cost too much. No one wanted to repeat the words of the younger, pre-imperialist Disraeli: colonies are like millstones around the home country's neck. Effective administration was therefore needed not only for assurance of local peace but also for collection of taxes and tariffs.

Given their limited funds and limited purposes, most colonial administrations seldom introduced changes in pre-existing social or political structures which were extensive or fundamental. Rather they tended to impose from above an administrative and judicial grid which overlay pre-existing structures. Yet life on the local level was also touched. The orientation of local economies to European needs, the imposition of legal and fiscal policies on local populations, disturbed the old order, as did the simple but obvious presence of dominating foreigners. Yet, whatever his ambitions and dreams, the administrator on the local level was much more overseer than radical innovator.

To the merchant or entrepreneur, these new empires were essentially sources of raw materials, a means to the expropriation of natural resources needed in industrial Europe. In the long run modern empire did not pay nationally, that is, it did not enhance the well-being of the masses of citizens. But for some Europeans like Taubman Goldie in Nigeria or Cecil Rhodes in South Africa, or for some concerns like Unilever or Dutch Shell, empire was a handsomely paying proposition. Native wealth was made to flow outward, and the rewards generally went into the pockets of a few persons who were usually far removed from the jungle, savanna, or desert from which this wealth was taken.

Along with all the above remarks, which obviously

fall primarily into the category of criticism, goes one singularly important consideration about imperialism. The history of European overseas expansion, and most particularly that of its most recent phase, is the history of the initial transformation of the greater part of the world, its Westernization, or—to be less parochial—its modernization. While the forces of change were inherent in no particular cultural system, they were first channeled in Europe and from there were shipped out to the antipodes themselves. True, the masses under European control were most often haughtily ignored, but the Europeans were willing to initiate some of their native charges into the ways of the West, to confer upon them some of the cultural benefits abounding in Europe— even though the method they developed was one of harsh tutor and compliant pupil. This cultural minority, this native elite, in turn was to inspire the indigenous masses, to lead them to independence and, hopefully, to modernization. Yet, in another way the Europeans had prepared the way to modernization. To develop the economies of their possessions they had to build the rudiments of an "infrastructure," to grid the land with railroads, to mark the coastlines with deep-water ports, to cut through jungles and forests with roads. Although this labor of imperialism was done by Europeans, and although it generally attached the colonial economy to the dominating European one and not to the economies of adjacent territories, its results were a permanent asset to the land, beneficial ultimately to the colonized as well as to the colonizer.

17

🏴

The story of how the small appendage of the Eurasian land mass spread out to come to hold the four corners of the world in fee has considerable romance, adventure, and suspense. It has its swashbuckling episodes, its feats of heroism and dogged determination—need one say more than Gordon at Khartoum?—and its moments of mystery and glory. Unfortunately, it also has its evident marks of greed, mayhem, and brutality. The exploitation of the natives in Leopold's Congo, the South African policy of *apartheid*, and the Opium War in China comprise a sufficient catalogue of this. The whole thus becomes a complicated mesh of good and evil, of glory and vice. In truth, with the exception of early industrialism, no modern historical phenomenon has so encouraged historians to hurl moral invective. Dispassion to date has been a difficult state to arrive at, as the following words written in 1960 suggest:

All in all, the half-millennium of Western colonial imperialism is a bloody stain on the history of mankind, an unbroken chain of the worst crimes against humanity, a chain which even in the twentieth century saw new links forged in it.[6]

Like Jacob's coat, European imperialism, whatever its particular phase, appears in many colors, ranging from the Black Myth of Spanish colonial administration in South America to the Red Myth of capitalist exploitation in Africa and Asia. Yet, despite its theoretical interpretations, its global range and its historical variety, European overseas imperialism does reveal one general pat-

[6] Alexander Ruestow, "The Remnants of Western Imperialism: a German View," *Review of Politics*, XXII (January 1960), 48.

18

tern. From beginning to end it was based on mercantile economic policy and on external political domination. Like the European state system with which it was so closely connected, it arose at a time when markets were expanding and political power was being consolidated. Colonies were then seen as a source of economic wealth which could be used to enhance political power. When the new imperialism of the late nineteenth century again propelled the European states across the seas, the state system was entering its mature phase. Fear of rival power again led to the belief that colonies would enhance political power. Power politics and commercial policy were the real forces behind European imperialistic expansion. While the balance between the two varied— and it never was susceptible to fine measurement—these are the constant factors whatever the period.

The major transformations in modern empire were generally of an administrative sort touching on economic and social matters and generally bundled together in what was called, in acceptable nineteenth-century parlance, "native policy." From the infamous slave trade in Africa and the plantation system in the New World, when the Negro was treated as chattel, until the final devolution of empire when he was no longer described as a "native" but addressed as "monsieur" or "sir," variations in administrative policy suggest some sort of evolutionary process. Particularly in the early twentieth century, policy reflected a growing sense of responsibility on the part of the European colonial administrators; and in that same period a growing awareness of their particular disadvantages was registered by the indigenous populations. The intersection of these two "growth curves" occurred in the post-World War II era when overseas imperialism was seen as an anachronism and was thus swept away by a new wave of nationalism.

What will certainly be one of the most striking aspects of the history of this imperialism when viewed a millennium hence will be the unusual time span it had. If one allows 1492 to stand as a convenient date with which to begin the first phase of it and 1776 as a convenient date with which to end it, nearly three hundred years, a solid chunk of historical time, elapsed. Again, if one allows 1877—the year Stanley completed his exploration of the Congo River—as another convenient initial date, and 1957—the year of Ghana's independence—as another terminal date, the second phase of that imperialism endured only eighty years, a rather short historical period by anyone's standard. Yet it is the shorter span of imperialism which was the more meaningful. Then hundreds of millions of people, hitherto unacquainted with the West and its technology, were made aware of the ways of the modern world. Railroads, electricity, health measures— and taxes—entered and complicated their lives. Toward the end of the imperialistic age, a "revolution of rising expectations" swept the globe. This was an anticipation of the benefits and satisfactions yet to come once independence had been obtained. The European first aroused this anticipation, even if he never genuinely satisfied it.

Over the seas and far away European imperialists intruded into old and honorable civilizations. They did so imperiously and cavalierly. They overturned thoughtlessly; they discarded haughtily; they destroyed callously. They also awakened and initiated. Even Nehru concedes this point in *Toward Freedom:*

Science was the great gift of the West; India lacked this, and without it she was doomed to decay. The manner of our contacts was unfortunate and yet, perhaps, only a succession of violent shocks could shake us out of our torpor.

However crude and unpleasant the process, this is the way One World, the modern world, began.

2 . THE EARLY EXPANSION OF EUROPE

Men have always gone down to the sea in ships. They have trafficked, adventured, and fought on the waters of the world and so have made them the greatest means of social contact and conflict that history has ever known. Yet the vast expanses of ocean were sufficiently forbidding to discourage European navigation far from the sight of land until recent centuries. Worldly ignorance combined with technological insufficiency to make sailing hazardous, and thus expeditions to *terra incognita* were rare.

At the time of the Renaissance, however, European interests became more dominantly secular, so that this world and man's place in it occupied the attention of the learned, who now observed earthly horizons and heavenly vistas with more discernment. Discovery thereupon became less accidental and more prepared, with improved instruments of navigation and better-rigged ships making sailing a more practical science. Then, for the first time in Western European history, considerable numbers of explorers set out to determine the nature and extent of the earth; adventurers set out to seize and exploit the wealth of the earth; and missionaries set out to assure that all those who lived on the earth would be afforded the opportunity of enjoying heavenly bliss. Along with this varied troupe went the stalwart colonists who settled chiefly in North America.

The impressive list of all their exploits has produced a plethora of volumes on the romance of empire: with Magellan around the world, with Captain Cook in the South Pacific, with La Salle on the Mississippi; the courage of the Jesuits and the Puritans in the New World, the naval exploits of Albuquerque in the Indian Ocean, the stubborn tenacity and hearty endeavors of the Dutch in the Cape of Good Hope. It was a great age of discovery, that historical moment when the narrow confines of coastal Europe were thrown open, with oceans becoming broad avenues to new and exotic worlds. To paraphrase the French historian Michelet, the Europe of the Renaissance was the age when man discovered himself and the universe.

The motives of the sea-fancying Europeans may have seemed nearly as varied as the lands to which they directed themselves. Yet if one had to distinguish in importance among the three elements of the famous trilogy summing up colonial objectives—God, gold, and glory —gold would stand out by far. The initial European impetus to empire certainly had its Christian crusading aspects, but it was primarily derived from the search for new routes to the wealth of the East. The opulence of Cathay and the valued spices of the Archipelago—as later the silver and gold of the New World—enticed a Europe still working on the preconditions necessary for what W. W. Rostow has called the "take-off" stage to self-sustaining economy. As ships became larger and as opportunities for cutting into the spice trade became smaller, the late arrivals in the imperialist race, England and France, turned to trade in bulk goods, both in India and on the North American continent. Later they were joined by the Dutch, who added coffee and rice to their hitherto exotic list of Eastern products. Trade thus increased in volume as it increased in variety, but everywhere a quantitative imbalance continued to exist: more went into Europe than came out. The Workshop of the World had yet to be founded.

Certain modern writers, notably from Africa, have argued that the West incurred an obligation to the present-day underdeveloped countries when it invaded them and ravaged them economically. The wealth taken from these regions hundreds of years ago, they contend, was the source of capital and materials which made the industrialization, hence the modernization, of Europe possible. Not only was it precious metals that were taken, but also it was the lives of millions of Negroes exported as chattel from Africa. Liverpool, it has been said more than once, was built on the bones of slaves.

It would be a sure denial of historical evidence to suggest that colonial enterprise did not give a great spurt to European economies. By the eighteenth century the trade routes from the New World to the east were heavily burdened with the wealth that was to enrich a hitherto underdeveloped Europe. Empire did pay, as the foreign trade statistics of England, Holland, and France amply reveal. Tobacco, timber, furs, and sugar from the New World; cotton, spices, and silk from Asia; and slaves, ivory, and gold from Africa all fell into European hands and filled European coffers.

The economic theory with which this imperialist expansion became identified is called mercantilism. Eli Heckscher, in his now classical study, *Mercantilism*, described this as economic policy with political objectives. "All economic activity," he wrote, was to be "subservient to the state's interest in power." Mercantilism was one of the means by which the European political units were expanded from regional and provincial centers of power into dynastic and national states. Certainly the relationship between these states and imperialism is obvious. Without his empire in the New World, Philip II of Spain could never have indulged in his endless military and diplomatic forays on the continent. His father, Charles V, who waged war against the French king, Francis I, had soon aroused in the latter the desire to find "golden bullets," his euphemism for the colonial gold and silver mines which were made to pay the heavy costs of

Charles's *Machtpolitik*. Seen from the prevailing European political perspective, the wealth of the world overseas was important to the aggrandizement of state power. If not earlier, certainly by the early eighteenth century, everywhere imperialist activities became significant extensions of European politics. The so-called Second Hundred Years' War, which pitted England against France at the end of the seventeenth century and throughout the eighteenth, actually consisted of several European wars which had colonial counterparts. The most influential of them was the Seven Years' War, 1756–1763, which in truth was initiated by its colonial counterpart, the French and Indian War in Canada.

The German historian Ludwig Dehio, in his seminal study, *The Precarious Balance*, suggests the close correlation between European and colonial activities. Analyzing the European power system within its world context, he argues that the "flanking" regions of the world—the Ottoman Empire, the Spanish Empire, and later the Dutch and English Empires, for instance—were made to bear heavily on European continental politics. His thesis in brief is that these regions were counterweights by which the balance, that is, the political equilibrium, of Europe could be maintained. In their day the colonial regions served in a capacity similar to that of the United States and the Soviet Union in helping right European affairs in World War II. Something of the idea of the "New World redressing the Old" permeates Dehio's thought.

Dehio's historical canvas is large, his strokes sweeping. Yet his essential idea bears further examination. The rise of European overseas expansion along with the rise of the European state system is more than coincidental. As a significant generalization, one can assert that overseas imperialism received its rhythm from that of the European state system. Empire waxed and waned as did Europe, rising first in those halcyon days when Tudor England became a naval power, the burgomasters of Amsterdam monopolized the carrying trade, and Louis XIV tried to make the world radiate in his sun. The convenience of 1492 as the date upon which to peg the start of European expansion is obvious. The date has the particular advantage of being not only the year in which Columbus sailed the ocean blue but also the year in which the Moors were finally expelled from Spain, thus allowing it to coalesce into a nation. With nationhood in Spain and the rest of Europe soon came the primacy of politics. The old *res publica christiana* which tried to affirm the necessary ascendancy of the religious over the secular, the Church over the State, was in a condition of collapse. The Church's gross involvement in Italian politics, the fission created by Protestantism, the doubts raised by humanistic studies were all disadvantages to any ecumenical religious principle. As the Christian world declined, and with it moral strictures on political activity, the secular world arose. The concept of *raison d'état*—the well-being of the state before any other consideration—became the cardinal principle of the European state system. As Machiavelli wrote in *The Prince*, the first rule of statesmanship was a firm grasp on power. Among other things the wise ruler had to be provident, had to build dikes against future floods which might sweep down upon him. Using Machiavelli's metaphor, we can say that colonies were made to serve as the dikes, as supports of national power when the nation was confronted with rising aggressive rivals.

While the theory explaining this growing interrelationship of political and economic power was labeled mercantilism, it also has been called Colbertism, an unmerited honor bestowed upon Jean-Baptiste Colbert, Louis XIV's devoted finance minister. Colbert's ideas were not original; they followed upon a long procession of mercantile thought coming from Frenchmen like Richelieu, from Dutchmen like John De Witt, and from Englishmen like Raleigh. Moreover, Colbert was much less the theorist than the determined administrator. The imperialist endeavors in which he engaged, however, were done in the service of France's mightiest king and were of great importance, as was the financial purpose behind them. All aspects considered therefore, this particular "ism" may not be entirely out of place.

Colbert was chiefly interested in the financial well-being of the kingdom he served. To assure this condition he believed that France had to export more than she imported—the concept of a favorable balance of trade. In this manner her gold reserves would be increased, not depleted, for her dependency on other countries would be minimal. This desired objective could be attained only by guaranteeing to France sources of the supplies she needed and by guaranteeing that all French merchandise would be transported in French ships. In Colbert's day this policy was called *L'Exclusif*, exclusive trading of colony with mother country. As a policy it rested on the assumption that the primary purpose of the colonies was to serve the mother country. One author has therefore asserted that Colbert was really not a colonialist at all, so limited was his view of overseas expansion.[1] Colbert's own words in a letter to the director of the West India Company dated September 6, 1673, support the contention:

> I will continue to tell you that you should have no other view in that country but that of commerce, that you should do everything possible to know well the merchandise which can be marketed in Europe . . . in a word, do everything with the true and singular spirit of commerce.

Colbertism, or mercantilism, was preached and followed with varying degrees of intensity and success by other European states running from Sweden to Spain. It was the form practiced by Spain which was the earliest and most aggravated, however. The riches of the New World, laying heavily in the hulls of the yearly treasure fleet plying the seas to Cádiz, were filtered through that monopolist clearing house, the Casa de Contratación, and made to support the Spanish economy. The simplistic thought behind this policy—that precious metals *ipso facto* mean national wealth—was based on abysmal ignorance of the function of industry and trade. The results of this policy can be summed up in a bimetallic metaphor: the Golden Age of Spain, based on New World silver, soon tarnished. No nation in history has

[1] Charles-André Julien, "Colbert," in Ch.-A. Julien et R. Delavignette, *Les Constructeurs de la France d'outre-mer* (Paris, 1946), p. 126.

rivaled the ability of Hapsburg Spain to impoverish itself with riches.

Far more sensible and temperate in approach was English mercantilism, a policy which seemed sound for its day and which helped England along the royal road to maritime and commercial success. In the 1630's Thomas Mun wrote his well-read and now famous *England's Treasure by Forraign Trade*, in which he summed up the prevailing thought succinctly: "The ordinary means . . . to increase our wealth and treasure is by Forraign Trade, where wee must ever observe this rule: to sell more to strangers than wee consume of theirs in value."

Mercantilist policy was a combination of certain ingredients, the weight of which varied according to the European power engaged: favorable balance of trade, bullionism, colonial enterprise, naval power.

All aspects of this policy were premised on the assumption that the amount of the world's resources was limited. Modern theories of economic growth were unknown to the theorists of the seventeenth and eighteenth centuries—prior to Adam Smith, at least. Theirs was conceived of as a static universe with fixed properties and fixed quantities. Like the system of political balance of power, there was an imagined system of economic balance of power. If one wished to add to his own economic resources, this had to be done by subtracting from those of someone else. Maintenance of exclusive trade with colonies, introduction of navigation acts requiring that all national goods be carried in ships flying that nation's flag, protective tariff policies; these were all expressions of this basic economic premise.

Before mercantilism reached its polished theoretical form in the seventeenth century, the efforts at imperialism were more often than not initiated by private groups rather than European states. The Spanish conquistador, the Dutch merchant, and the English Puritan, each in his own way and with his own purpose, set sail and carved out a bit of empire, perhaps with the benevolent nod of governmental authorities but seldom with more than that. The form through which this private initiative was most frequently expressed was the company financed principally by the device of joint stock and legally sanctioned principally by a royal charter. These companies were not, however, only commercial enterprises as we now know them. Of necessity they sooner or later became involved in governmental activities. To secure trade treaties, to establish entrepôts and factories on foreign territory, to administer to the needs of resident European populations, and to protect themselves against the incursions of greedy European rivals, the companies needed diplomatic skills, powers of government, and some military might. In the New World the English chartered companies were endowed with the essential elements of representative government. Not responsible to the Crown through royally appointed governors, as were their equivalents in French Canada, these colonial companies enjoyed the right to elect their own officers by and from the freeholders within the company. In the East the political role of the companies was more reluctantly assumed. The directors of the Dutch East India Company were interested only in trade at good profit and declined from the acquisition of empire. But the governors on the scene soon learned, as had Albuquerque before them, that to secure trade some political control of the land surrounding the trading post had to be secured. By the end of the eighteenth century the Dutch had laid the foundation for a large political empire in the Indonesian archipelago, and to the west of them the English merchant company, known as the East India Company, was doing the same, thanks primarily to the unusual energies of one of its administrators, Robert Clive.

The freedom these companies at times enjoyed in their heyday was not long left unimpaired. By the end of the seventeenth century the state tended to intervene and to control them. Either the political and military tasks thrust upon the companies were beyond their capacities, or they proved to be financially insolvent, or in fulfilling their tasks they tended to exceed their chartered authority. With the Restoration of the Stuart monarchy in England attempts were made to place the North American chartered companies directly under Crown authority with the appointment of royal governors. As early as 1638 the king of France sent a governor to the Antilles charged to watch over the French company there established and "to safeguard the rights of His Majesty." By 1674 the French Company of the West Indies was so unsuccessful that its territories were directly annexed to the Crown. Finally, Parliament came to gain control over the affairs of the British East India Company initially through Pitt's India Act of 1784.

While experimented with again in the late nineteenth century, the chartered company as a primary vehicle of colonial trade and expansion became more the exception than the rule. Hereafter the state became more immediately and directly involved. It most often initiated imperialism and did not generally follow, or hide behind, private enterprise. In the sixteenth and seventeenth centuries, when state wealth and power were only beginning to be accumulated, the chartered company was a useful device by which the government obtained revenue, increased trade, and founded colonies, all the while retaining a maximum of freedom of political action and a minimum of political involvement. In the seventeenth century colonial rivalry and its ill effects could be overlooked as a *casus belli;* the Dutch and English did not go to war when the Duke of York annexed New Amsterdam and renamed it New York, for example. In the eighteenth century colonial rivalry often aggravated European affairs and appeared as a *casus belli*. The European state system was beginning to operate; dynastic and national interests were emerging as paramount; and the "balance of power" was the *modus operandi*, however crude and clumsy it now appears to have been.

An overemphasis can be placed on the significance of European power politics in their world setting. No impression should be given of an all-powerful European state easily and quickly moving outward where it would. As mentioned before, Europe in the early period of imperialist expansion was still underdeveloped, or better, did not have a tremendous edge on the rest of the world. Although possessed of firearms, seaworthy ships, and horses, the European expansionists did not always enjoy a measurable preponderance of power. In sparsely populated regions like North America they could secure a firm footing and settle permanently. In regions where the population was docile or somewhat indifferent, as in Latin America, they could make conquest a quick, if bloody, enterprise. Elsewhere their stay was dependent on the pleasure or cooperation of the local government. They resided in China thanks to the benign attitude of the Manchu emperors; they traded in Western India under the shadow and protection of the so-called Mogul Empire of the early eighteenth century. They had not yet been able to open the door to Japan; and they found it nearly impossible and most disadvantageous to penetrate into the western interior of Africa where the coastal slaving states, like Dahomey, were strong enough, thanks to the trade in arms, to defend themselves. The European balance of power had not yet become a world balance of power in which Europe weighed most heavily. This political phenomenon only occurred during the hundred years separating the independence of America from the partition of Africa.

During this interval the outlines of territorial empires were being sketched. The eighteenth and nineteenth centuries were the age of the great land explorations, as the sixteenth and seventeenth centuries had been the age of the great sea explorations. The fluvial systems of North and Latin America and of Africa were being investigated and thus were to provide the means of European interior penetration. The growth of population would make the staffing of an empire a much easier task. (Compare the Portuguese Empire supported by a population of 4,000,-000 at home with that of Imperial Germany with a population of 60,000,000 at home.) And, of course, the effects of industrialization would give Europe a material superiority.

All of this said, one can still marvel at the extent of early empire and the relative ease with which it was acquired. What accounts for this? Without trying to evaluate them in order of significance, the following are usually presented as the essential reasons. European firepower and nautical skills were superior to those of the peoples encountered. Albuquerque's successes against the Arab and Egyptian fleets provide an obvious example. European horsemanship in Latin America helped considerably in Cortez' conquest of Mexico with a band of only several hundred men. The religious zealousness and the lust for loot and trade which inspired the Europeans were important psychological factors. Furthermore, internecine war and trade rivalry among the natives helped foster the European cause as one native prince or chief would try to ally with the European in an effort to dispose of a rival. The Dutch took advantage of the political rivalries in the Archipelago to sign a number of advantageous treaties of protectorate. Finally, and of great importance, the resident populations too often looked upon the Europeans as boorish and barbarian interlopers whose presence would be ephemeral and insignificant and who might be disposed of if desired. Even in the nineteenth century a high official of the Chinese Empire, Lin Tse-hsü, could condescendingly address Queen Victoria as if she lived on the periphery of the world.

By guile, daring, and determination, and by arms and seamanship, Europe acquired a maritime empire that was of great advantage to the political and economic growth of that continent.

The colonial empires were never simple appendages of the Old World. Whatever their established purpose in the minds of European politicians and merchants, they had their own existence. And they posed their own problems. What were the relations to be established between colonist abroad and countryman at home? What were the relations to be established between colonist and native? These questions aroused considerable concern, although the answers arrived at were never so satisfactory as those given to the same questions in the early twentieth century.

The relations between colonist and homeland varied considerably from colony to colony, but nowhere were they truly satisfactory. Removed by an ocean from central political control, the colonists were out of contact for months on end with the affairs of the homeland. Moreover, situated in frontier territories and often faced with hostility from indigenous populations, the colonists found themselves confronted with problems which were completely alien to the metropolitan mind. Then, conquistador and aspirant merchant prince found governmental regulations and justice restraints to their ruthless desire for quick wealth and power. Finally, as mercantilism became the prevalent doctrine, the colonists resented being subordinate to the economic wishes of the mother country.

The oldest of the political empires was that which Spain established in the New World. As free-lancing soldiers ravaged the land and as pious Dominican friars sought to convert where the soldier sought to kill, the Spanish monarchy and the able Spanish legists of the day genuinely tried to find a system of government and of jurisprudence which would best serve the interests of the Crown and of the local populations. Direct control was deemed the best, and the monarch, enjoying the title of "King of the Indies and the Lands of the Ocean Sea," appointed governors and viceroys responsible to him. Courts of appeal—*audiencias*—were established as trustworthy institutions of the Crown and as dispensers of impartial justice. They were staffed by well-trained jurists and helped provide a necessary corrective to conquistador excess. From the settler's point of view the municipality with its town council provided a means by which to raise a voice against the Crown when necessary and a means by which to maintain some political control. Although seriously criticized in later years, the Spanish colonial system was one of the most sincere and studied efforts to provide the colonies and the colonists with sound government.

Perhaps compared with the British activities in North America, the history of Spanish America seems uninspiring. The development of autonomous government in the North has been intensively studied, greatly commented upon, and generously praised—partly because these settlement colonies were the most significant, having a population of over 2,000,000 on the eve of the American Revolution, and partly because the results of British policy were so dramatic. In the beginning Crown control was tenuous. The proprietary colonies, such as those of Maryland or Pennsylvania, gave to their owner the right to dispose of the land as he saw fit and to be his own ruler; like a vast estate, they were ruled according to the wishes of their owner. The chartered colonies, such as that of Massachusetts, enjoyed the privileges of representative government and appointed their own governors. This system, while approved in the seventeenth century, was to prove a source of annoyance to the Crown in the eighteenth, when mercantile policy led to the attempt to subordinate the chartered colony to the will of the mother country. During the period of the Stuart Restoration attempts were made to strengthen the hold of the Crown over these colonies, with the result that in almost all of them governors were appointed by and made responsible to the Crown.

While the attempts at political consolidation of empire were being made by England, the North American colonies were coming into their own; they had reached a certain political maturity in the course of the eighteenth century, and hence they wished the responsibility commensurate with such status. Now "the presence of representative institutions was joined with the absence of responsible government."[2] To redress this problem, to

[2] Sir Ernest Barker, *Ideas and Ideals of the British Empire* (Cambridge, 1941), p. 74.

gain a firmer control over their own political destinies, many of the American colonists believed revolution was the only solution.

In the French North American possessions settlement was more sporadic, authority more strict, than in the English possessions. No comparable development toward autonomous rule occurred here, for the absolute monarchy tried to maintain its power absolutely. For instance, Colbert remonstrated when the Count de Frontenac, governor of Canada, called together in 1672 a local assembly representing the three estates. "Our kings have for some time considered it in their best interests not to call together the Estates-General of their kingdom," Colbert tartly wrote. The companies by which Colbert wielded the power of his empire were far more under Crown control than the English. Not only did the monarch provide much of the capital—however reluctant Louis XIV might have been to do this—but also he appointed most of the directors. For Colbert the companies were simply extensions of the state. Yet, despite this state apparatus, according to one authority, "Canada under the absolute monarchy was a democracy in practice." [3] While all power resided in the appointed governor, responsible to the monarch alone, the notables of the colony were consulted in most significant matters. Then, given the vastness of the land and the sparsity of the population, Frenchmen like the *coureurs de bois* enjoyed that certain liberty which went with such open frontiers.

[3] Hubert Deschamps, *Methodes et doctrines coloniales de la France* (Paris, 1953), p. 59.

Nevertheless, the French settlement empire in the north like the Spanish in the south never provided the opportunity for colonial political growth that did the English.

Viewed across the several centuries in which they developed, the political relationships between colonists and mother country reveal no constant or planned evolution. The European powers never displayed any sensitive or sustained interest in settlers' problems. The chief concerns were always so European-centered that colonial matters were seldom seen as being other than subordinate to the interests of the mother country. With the success of mercantile policy and the growing political and trade rivalry of the eighteenth century, this sentiment became more intransigent. For most of the colonial powers the early settlement colonies were lost before reform could be effected, even if it was deemed necessary. Canada was whisked away by the British at the end of the Seven Years' War; the effects of the Napoleonic Wars and the great energy of Simon Bolivar caused the Spanish colonial empire in South America to collapse at once. While the British alone responded seriously to colonial needs, they never responded sufficiently. The drastic innovations were introduced by the colonists themselves, particularly when they broke away in the War of Independence.

The French philosopher-economist Turgot once commented that colonies, like fruit, would fall from the tree when ripe. In a sense many of the settlement colonies had ripened. By the end of the eighteenth century they became detached, that is, disinterested in or hostile to the concerns of the mother country. Theirs was, as it almost had to be, a world removed from the daily concourse of old Europe. This few European statesmen could appreciate, and with dogged determination they continued their belief in mercantilism. Verbal assaults by free-trade advocates like Turgot and Adam Smith were without serious effect on official thinking. Reform in the remaining settlement colonies only came later, with the nineteenth century and the evolution of the British possessions, notably Canada, to the status of dominions. But even immediately following upon 1776 few English politicians or theorists looked in that particular direction.

The second question still remains: what was the relationship established between colonist and native? A simple and not untruthful answer would be that there seldom was one. In the trading empires of the East, the colonial-native relations were generally workaday, those of tradesmen given to haggling and bargaining. When they were not, they were outright aggressive, as in Albuquerque's sea duels with the Arabs, or as with the Java "culture system" through which natives were forced to grow crops for Dutch trade. Generally, real cultural contact in this part of the world was sporadic; it was never systematized or dignified with a policy.

In the New World settlement empires the story is not much more detailed. Extermination and enslavement seem to be the unfortunate key words. Land was acquired by pushing scattered populations back; work was done by impressment; concern for the native was minimal. Yet it is true that the religious enthusiasm which carried Catholic missionaries abroad to South America was channeled into a native policy. Men like Bartolomé de Las Casas believed in the equal latent ability of native and European and sought to engender a spirit of respect for and interest in the Indian populations. He and others like him sought to learn native dialects, to appreciate native ways in order to convert the indigenous population to the religion they believed to be so beneficial. The proselytism and spiritual democracy of Catholicism —a soul in every man—guided these efforts, and, as recent scholarship has shown, this native policy was an enlightened one.[4]

The Spanish effort notwithstanding, there was no really extensive and carefully contrived native policy in the colonial world. As is well known, the Portuguese carried their religious ideas abroad as did the Spanish, and their efforts were even crowned with unusual but momentary success when in the early seventeenth century one of the rulers of Ethiopia converted to Catholicism. Elsewhere, the French in Canada were moving toward a policy of cultural assimilation, as Colbert's suggestion that the French and Indians "form a single people" reveals. Still, by and large, very little serious attention was paid to the needs and demands of the peoples over whom the Europeans now had control.

Interestingly enough, on the periphery of empire, in China, India, and Turkey, the European of the seventeenth and eighteenth centuries was fascinated and frequently awed by what he observed. He became introspective as he made comparisons with other lands and

[4] See particularly Louis Hanke, *The First Social Experiments in America: A Study in the Development of Spanish Indian Policy in the Sixteenth Century* (Cambridge, Mass., 1935).

often found his own civilization dull or less than satisfactory. This genuine openmindedness was matched across the Atlantic by the popular myth of the Noble Savage—that carefree, unharried North American Indian who communed with nature. A popular topic of discussion in European salon society, the Noble Savage never suffered inferiority with the contemporary European as long as he remained *in abstracto;* in reality his fate was never so fair.

Tragically, the closest and most enduring contacts between Europeans and non-Europeans in this first phase of overseas imperialism were made in the course of the African slave trade. To treat people as animals, to herd them into dingy and excessively crowded ships, the European slave trader had to be either calloused or self-deluding about the fate of these people. He tended to be both; first, considering only the cash nexus, the value of his cargo of ebony; and second, deeming the Negro to be inferior, given to cannibalism, and hence no worse off in chains—perhaps better—than in savage freedom in the jungles. In the African slave trade some of the deepest roots of racism grew, and in the African slave trade was provided one of the most outrageous examples of man's inhumanity to man.

From the eagle's heights the first phase of overseas expansion, while covering four centuries, seems not to have made the impression that its successor of the late nineteenth century was to. Of course the migration of the white population to the four corners of the world was a major historical event, and the opening up of the world to European trade can hardly be matched. Yet in the strict terms of political and territorial empire, what one sees is an outline, an adumbrated form of the vast annexations of territories and peoples which in the nineteenth century was to make Europe all but master of the world. Furthermore, in this early phase colonial forms of government and native policy were left undeveloped. Very little sense of responsibility toward empire evolved intelligently in European court or governmental circles. Writing of the Dutch in the East Indies, one author has this to say: "Merchants they were and scarcely conscious of other concepts than those of money and profit." [5] What was said of the Dutch could as easily be said of most other colonial peoples. Imperialism appeared to be a quick and rather easy source to considerable wealth; it was a means by which to fill the king's treasury, to pay for his armies, to allow him to enjoy a grand foreign policy. It was also the source of private financial gain, as men like the "nabobs" returned from India, having mulcted the land and the East India Company sufficiently to purchase handsome country estates far from the madding crowd. Marx, with his apt ability to employ striking phraseology, called these empires "plundering empires." They were very close to being just that.

Most significant of all, this first wave of European expansion initially opened the world to the West. It established an attitude and a practice which were not to be forgotten in the following centuries. And it indicated the ability of Europe to turn the world to its own interests.

[5] J. J. Van Klaveren, *The Dutch Colonial System in the East Indies* (The Hague, 1953), p. 39.

The old colonial system may have decayed in the late eighteenth century and the early nineteenth. Free-trade doctrines, the distracting activities of continental wars, and the pressing demands for domestic political and social reform in the age of industrialism may have caused attention to be diverted from the attractions of empire. But imperialism did not therefore stop; no country willingly divested itself of empire, and few countries were able to resist the urge to empire when it once again was felt.

3 . THE NEW RUSH OVERSEAS

Toward the end of the nineteenth century the recrudescence of imperialism occurred, leading to the so-called Scramble for Africa and the nearly final consumption of the remaining noncolonial territories of Asia. Until quite recently, this series of events was analyzed as sudden and new, an outburst after a hiatus of one hundred years of noncolonial, nonimperialist activity. Now historical analysis has shown otherwise.[1] Imperialism was scarcely

[1] The principal presentation of this argument is Ronald Robinson and John Gallagher, "The Imperialism of Free Trade," *The Economic History Review*, VI, No. 1 (1953), 1–15.

quiescent during the lengthy interval separating the American Revolution from Stanley's exploration of the Congo. The most familiar form it then assumed, however, was indirect, essentially economic predominance with none of the heavy responsibilities of direct administration. Nevertheless, in this very same period sporadic outbursts of direct imperialism were easily discernible, as witness the French in Algeria and the Senegal or the British in Burma and above all in India. What occurred at the end of the nineteenth century, then, was new only in its intensity, but this alone is sufficient to cause it to be singled out. At no time before or since has "earth hunger" seemed more voracious—or more completely satisfied.

What drove Europe out with such gusto has been a question asked many times over and provided with an impressive array of answers. There is no need to try to sort these all out, however, for the pattern of this phase of imperialism seems very clear in retrospect.

No matter from what angle observed, the effort appears as a national one. Whether begun by merchant, adventurer, or soldier; whether extolled in religious, sociological, or racial terms, empire was established and maintained by nationalistic European states and directly through their responsible agencies. An appreciation of this new imperialism, therefore, can best be gained by first observing the political setting in which these nation-states acted.

With the unification of Germany and Italy in 1870–1871 the European state system appeared complete. A grouping of independent states, still operating on the principle of balance of power, the system was dynamic, characterized by manipulation and maneuvering, by the exercise of aggressive diplomacy and the assertion of national rights and prerogatives. Unlike its seventeenth- and eighteenth-century predecessor, the late nineteenth-century system was aggravated by a chauvinistic, exclusivist nationalism which suggested that state rivalry was a necessary condition of political life, and which found pseudo-scientific support in the social Darwinian notions of struggle for survival and survival of the fittest. Fear, not complacency; anxiety, not confidence characterized international politics at the end of the nineteenth century, as each country viewed its neighbors' strength with growing concern. The condition of European peace therefore resulted not from relaxation, but from tension. It was the effect of "an equivalent development of power" according to the German historian Friedrich Meinecke.

Admiral Mahan described the situation as "an equilibrium on the Continent, and, in connection with the calm thus resulting, an immense colonizing movement in which all the great powers were concerned." The exciting and daring political activity was now undertaken outside of Western Europe. New zones of friction developed and old ones were intensified: the Middle East, North Africa and Africa south of the Sahara, Southeast Asia. The growing realization of the possible political and economic worth of Africa and Asia to the European states directed national attention thither. Fervid nationalists took new hope in the possibilities of national grandeur and expressed themselves in terms of a "Greater Britain," a *Plus Grande France*, and a *Gross Deutschland*. Active colonial policy seemed a means to renewed national success, a source of new power and world significance. France, recovering from the humiliating defeat by Prussia in 1870, wished to regild her renown abroad. Germany, until recently dismembered, wished to break out of the political encirclement which she imagined to exist and to be a check to her *Weltpolitik*. Italy, also unified and thinking in terms of a Third Rome, dreamed occasionally of Roman Africa. And Great Britain, sensing her relative decline in a world of new great powers, notably the United States and Germany, derived some solace from the notion of an empire upon which the sun never set.

A flood of political epigrams describing the urgency and glory of imperialistic actions came from the pens of the proponents of empire. "Colonization is for France a matter of life or death," wrote the French colonial theorist Leroy-Beaulieu. The German foreign minister, Prince von Bülow, remarked in a phrase now notorious: "We do not want to put anyone in the shade, but we demand a place for ourselves in the sun." And in a fit of patriotic and poetic verve, Cecil Rhodes intoned: "I would annex the planets if I could."

Soon the European nations again fanned out into the world, hoping that size and breadth of acquisition would assure them leadership or favorable location in this comity of competitive nations. With choice irony,

Joseph Conrad's hero Marlowe in *Heart of Darkness* observed the pictorial effects of this effort as he looked at the map of Africa:

There was a vast amount of red—good to see at any time, because one knows that some real work is done there, a deuce of a lot of blue, a little green, smears of orange, and, on the East Coast, a purple patch to show where the jolly pioneers of progress drink the jolly lager beer.

This colorful activity was politically directed, but its success depended on that awesome *ultima ratio*, power. Just as the major underlying cause of Europe's political unrest was the immense military and economic power that the states were amassing, so the dreams of empire were easily realized by the utilization of this power. In short, the urge to political empire and the realization of such empire can be paired only where the physical means of domination are available. Thus, while one can aver that the new phase of imperialism was the undertaking of the European nation-state, he is obliged to explain the particular nature of national power and the uses to which it was put so as to distinguish it from that which was earlier existent. The qualitative and quantitative differences between the power at the disposal of the sixteenth-century Portuguese and that available to the nineteenth-century Germans, for instance, are of great significance in explaining the rapidity and extent of modern imperialism.

Europe was the first of the world's regions to modernize: to amass, organize, and dispose of its human and natural resources in such a way that human needs were rather easily satisfied and human power was increased manifold. Primarily a nineteenth-century phenomenon, this culturally revolutionary process was both caused by and resulted in the urban, industrial society which we all by common agreement now call "modern." The European political framework within which the process occurred was, of course, the national one, and the value system upon which it was structured emphasized secularism and rationalism: man's independence of fate and nature, his ability to understand and control the world in which he lives. For the first time in history ideas, techniques, and institutions were mobilized in such a way that one small region of the world enjoyed a material cultural superiority that necessitated not comparison but contrast with the many civilizations that were oceans and seas removed from it.

It is in the nature of this contrast that the causes and success of modern imperialism are to be found. The asymmetrical power relationship between Europe and the rest of the world not only made imperialism possible, it also made imperialism tempting. Empire could be acquired "on the cheap," and most often was. Superior military equipment made the subduing of foreign peoples no inordinately grave task. As Hilaire Belloc quipped:

> Whatever happens we have got
> The Maxim gun and they have not.

Superior means of transportation enabled empire to be consolidated and bound. The steam engine propelled the railroad trains that crossed new continents and the freighters which transported goods from empire to mother country and back again. Superior communications ensured greater imperial control: the telegraph became the new line of empire, allowing Whitehall, the Quai d'Orsay, and Wilhelmstrasse to listen in to the world abroad. Technology made the world one, and won most of the world for Europe.

Against this technological and organizational triumph, the economically underdeveloped regions of the world were quite helpless or indifferent. Overseas imperialism occurred only where power had ebbed, as in the decaying empires of Turkey, Moslem India, or China; or where power had never been effectively organized on a large-scale and rather permanent basis, as in parts of Africa. In brief, the new imperialism always involved striking contrasts of potential power. The adjective "potential" is significant, for the stronger power was not always wantonly used; it was often displayed symbolically, as in the form of a beplumed viceroy seated on a carpeted dais, or a mighty ship of war riding gracefully at anchor, or a railroad cutting purposively through jungle or desert. The ways of the West were impressive and were soon to be imitated.

Yet the very societal organization which brought Europe to its ascendancy over the rest of the world was also responsible for the urge toward empire and the intensity with which it was felt. As the European nations strengthened their national structures and became more aggressively nationalistic, and as their separate industrial economies seemed more and more bent on aggravated competition, particularly with the advent of the United States and Germany as great economic powers, the tendency toward national policies of trade protection was increased. In such an atmosphere fear of dwindling or closed foreign markets and sources of raw materials suggested the need for the acquisition of national economic preserves. "Without colonies, no more exportation," exclaimed the Frenchman Henri Mager, who almost seemed to be frantically replying to the statement made by United States Senator Albert J. Beveridge: "The trade of the world must be ours."

Such mercantile policy—"neo-mercantilism" it has been labeled by many commentators—reveals an obvious similarity to its seventeenth-century predecessor and implies again a close relationship between economics and politics. How to separate the two is a perplexing question to historians of the subject. However, thanks to the usual dialectics of historical debate, the major distinctions are easily found. At one extreme are those individuals, principally in the Hobson-Lenin tradition, who see modern imperialism as the result of capitalistic economics. To Hobson, in *Imperialism: A Study*, published first in 1902, imperialism principally occurred as a result of maldistribution in capitalist society. A surfeit of capital and goods, not absorbed in the home economy because of the lack of a more equitable distribution of wealth among the social classes, needed an international exit, and hence colonies and areas of domination were sought as places of investment. Trade and the flag went together, or as Hobson wrote:

It is this economic condition of affairs that forms the taproot of imperialism. If the consuming public in this country [England] raised its standard of consumption to keep pace with every rise of productive powers, there could be no excess of goods or capital clamorous to use imperialism in order to find markets. . . .

For Hobson the problem was not inherent in capitalistic society, for it was susceptible to correction. He was not unduly sanguine, however, about the ease with which the necessary change, to wit the real democratization of society, would be made. In his day imperialism was still displaying great vitality—it is "only beginning to realize its full force," he wrote—and society was far from completely reformed.

In *Imperialism: The Highest Stage of Capitalism*, Lenin viewed the matter differently, asserting that the developing structure of capitalism made imperialism an ineluctable economic necessity. Within his modified Marxist framework, imperialism was another, but the highest, stage of capitalism. The process which he described can be recapitulated in short measure. Capitalist competition had given way to monopolies; large investment banks had appeared and soon were enmeshed with industry in a financial net; great quantities of surplus capital were now accumulated, quantities which could be profitably invested abroad only in those regions where capital was in scarce supply. Along with goods, the capitalist countries now exported capital. In Lenin's own words:

Imperialism is capitalism in that stage of development in which the dominance of monopolies and finance capital has established itself; in which the division of the world among the international trusts has begun; in which the division of all territories of the globe among the great capitalist powers has been completed.

Throughout the period between the two world wars, when the traditional European political and economic order was assailed, variations of this economic interpretation of imperialism remained the most attractive ones, complete with their moral conclusions.

The results of the policy of economic imperialism pursued by this country [England] and the other imperialist powers can hardly be viewed with satisfaction or equanimity. Political subjection, exploitation, and economic slavery are never pleasant to their victims.

These words, written by the British Labourite Leonard Woolf in 1922, were not unusually severe.

In opposition to this position is found a series of more recent statements of the problem which de-emphasize or discard economic motivations. First and foremost among them is the opinion held by the Austrian economist Joseph Schumpeter, who described imperialism as essentially a militaristic problem. "History, in truth, shows us nations and classes—most nations furnish an example at some time or other—that seek expansion for the sake of expanding, war for the sake of fighting, victory for the sake of winning, dominion for the sake of ruling." From this Schumpeter concluded that "imperialism is the objectless disposition on the part of a state to unlimited forcible expansion." [2] Several more recent critics have

[2] Joseph Schumpeter, "Imperialism," in *Imperialism and Social Classes* (New York, 1958), p. 6.

placed imperialism in a political mold, thus eliminating Schumpeter's insistence on its "objectlessness." The French historian Henri Brunschwig has found French imperialism of the late nineteenth century to be the direct result of a recrudescence of nationalism, the concerted effort on the part of nationalist politicians to regain France's position of peerage within the circle of the European great powers.[3] Lastly, there is the opinion of two British scholars, Robinson and Gallagher, who have interpreted the partition of Africa as being essentially political. Speaking of the responsible English ministers of the period, these authors write: "Their territorial claims were not made for the sake of African empire or commerce as such. They were little more than by-products of an enforced search for better security in the Mediterranean and the East." It was England's Egyptian policy which precipitated the partition, they insist. Their conclusion: "So far from commercial expansion requiring the extension of territorial claims, it was the extension of territorial claims which in time required commercial expansion."[4]

Some analysts in this debate had already arrived at conclusions not dissimilar to those of Robinson and Gallagher. They thought the economic cause to be an *ex post facto* consideration, a means of convincing the voters and parliamentarians who controlled the nation's purse strings of the value of investing in the imperialist

[3] See Henri Brunschwig, *Mythes et réalités de l'impérialisme colonial français* (Paris, 1961).
[4] Ronald Robinson and John Gallagher, *Africa and the Victorians* (New York, 1961), pp. 463, 472.

game. There is much truth in this appraisal, particularly as it applies to French colonial policy. But to suggest that the economic argument was simply a device is to ignore the expansionist disposition of modern industrial economics. Of course, we now know that political empire is not a necessity for modern industrialism, capitalist or otherwise. The successful economic development of both Holland and France (not to mention Japan) in their postcolonial phase stands out as irrefutable contemporary proof. But to many late-nineteenth-century thinkers the economic value of imperialism was real and necessary: national markets did seem somewhat limited, industrial competition did seem pressing, and the Colbertian dictum about favorable balance of trade did have a contemporary ring. Yet if trade followed the flag on more than one occasion, the flag was not simply displayed to cover up the financial machinations of a capitalistic middle class. The outstanding proponents of imperialism were principally political visionaries who sought the way to national—political and economic—greatness. In general businessmen only responded to their urging at first; the taste for economic imperialism had to be acquired.

Lenin's thesis rested on the assumption that capital was attracted to the backward regions because of the high returns it would reap, thanks to the paucity of existing capital there—as opposed to the glut found in monopoly-ridden Europe—and thanks also to the availability of cheap labor. That money did flow outward and in enormous quantities, there is no denying, but this money did not head principally to the newly acquired regions of empire. The French in the years before World War I centered their financial activity first and foremost in Europe. Overseas, more money was invested in the United States and Latin America than in the colonies. The English in this same period held great investments in the United States but rapidly developed those in Latin America, Canada, Australia, and even India. As with France, England found her new empire no exceptionally attractive field for capital investment. The real imperialist *champs de manoeuvre* was Africa, and no enormous investment found its way there until after World War II, with the notable exception of South Africa, where mining absorbed considerable sums of capital. In short, there was no nice coincidence between new empire and new foreign investment which would suggest a close causal connection between the two. No pattern emerges which would support the idea that empire provided a financial safety valve for the capitalist machine.

The economic aspects of empire are not thus dispelled, however. The real value of the newly imperialized regions, at least as seen by the strong proponents of imperialism, was as trading areas first and as sources of raw material second. But the latter actually became the chief *raison d'être* as phosphates from North Africa, rubber and ivory from the Congo, hemp from Indochina, and oil from Indonesia all were fed into the gluttonous European industrial machine. Outside of the mining and petroleum industries, very few of these economic activities required great capital investment in order to be realized. Most of the products coming from the colonies were shipped out in a natural or semifinished state and hence needed very little expensive machinery or highly organized productive processes on the spot. It was in Europe where these products were refined and manufactured in already existing industrial complexes. As later critics were to complain, the world of empire was one of a neat division of labor: the colonies providing the raw materials, the colonial powers providing the industry; the former therefore remaining underdeveloped, the latter continuing to modernize.

In review, what conclusions might now be offered? Considered less in the form of history-as-event and more of history-as-process, modern imperialism is perhaps best described in terms of cultural relations, or more accurately, cultural conflict. Unlike earlier European imperialism, when the economic and political structures of colonizer and colonized were not markedly disparate, the difference between nineteenth-century Europe and those areas upon which it arbitrarily imposed its will was exceedingly great. It was the difference between a modern, urban, industrial culture resting on a rather popular base, and traditional, rural, agrarian cultures resting on an aristocratic base. The well-known dichotomy between traditional and modern states has particular relevance for this late-nineteenth-century era, one in which the transitional phase to modernity had not yet been thought of, let alone reached, for the vast non-European world.

European social processes had been so highly developed as a result of the political and industrial revolutions of the eighteenth and nineteenth centuries that European power, in almost whatever form, was vastly superior to that of any other region, with the notable exception of the United States, which for all practical purposes could be considered a part of this civilization. Very few were those areas which were able to resist the outward flow of European power. Japan is the striking example of a non-Western state that did this successfully and by means of a process of modernization which, ironically, enabled her to engage in a robust imperialism of her own.

Late-nineteenth-century imperialism was the most forceful and obvious manifestation of a modern society technologically advanced and nationalistically organized, a society capable of economic and political domination over much, indeed most, of the underdeveloped world. It was not the outcome of any historical necessity—Marxist or Social Darwinian. It was, however, the outcome of a combination of all-too-human concerns: fear of the power of surrounding states, personal and national ambitions for secular glory, the temptation to dominate the weak.

Despite the fact that imperialism was a conscious policy pursued by the state, it was the handiwork of a small number of enthusiasts, the prophets and politicians at home, the actors and movers abroad. Their vision may of course have been partially of personal gain—"philanthropy is good, but philanthropy at 5 per cent is better," said Rhodes—but it was more of national grandeur and prestige. They accomplished their work chiefly by the unpleasant means of intrigue and force, seizing territories, establishing protectorates, and signing treaties, all with next to no concern about the thoughts and desires of the resident populations. But they also accomplished their work cheaply. Until the Boer War and the Russo-Japanese War, imperial undertakings were not very costly in either men or equipment. Such undertakings may have outraged the consciences of the Socialists or disturbed parliaments from time to time; however, they occasioned no great popular outcries of national indignation and only infrequently gave cause for national alarm. On the contrary, they could and did arouse popular enthusiasm, "jingoism," to employ the favorite nineteenth-century term for the attitude. Only with the Boer War did an ardent debate over imperialism arise, but by then the general lines of colonial empire had been well defined.

As has been said before, in this age of rising nationalist passions which was the last quarter of the nineteenth century, empire was more of a comfort than an irritant, if it was seriously considered at all. And that it was all too seldom seriously—that is thoroughly—considered at the time is a point not without meaning.

Between European intentions and ambitions in pegging out claims to empire and the actual realization of that empire, there was considerable distance. In part this gap was due to the combination of arrogance and ignorance which frequently prevailed in the imperialist camp. Imperialists at home enthusiastically embraced the idea of empire *in abstracto* but too seldom revealed a well-founded knowledge of the territories in which this power was to dominate. Expressions like the Dark Continent and the Mysterious East were descriptive less of the lack of geographical familiarity on the part of the European than of the meager awareness of the social and historical developments of these lands. As a former cabinet minister of Malawi once said: "Stanley didn't discover us; we were here all the time." The cavalier attitude that sometimes accompanied such European ignorance can be gathered from Jules Ferry's comment that modern empire was "an immense steeplechase on the road of the unknown." Far from the scene of the action, European politicians, gathered in comfortably appointed chancelleries, carved out their empires with a pen.

Nevertheless, this does not mean that the geographical configurations of modern empire were the result either of historical accident or of diplomatic whim. The new imperialism was far from patternless. True, the real legwork—the surveying of the real estate—was done by men who sought fame and fortune abroad, who often wished to escape the seemingly humdrum existence of bourgeois Europe. But unlike their predecessors in the Age of Discovery, they enjoyed no immense freedom of action. In general the European powers knew where they were expanding, even if they did not know what their territories contained.

Most of the empires tended to extend from pre-existing bases. What happened in the Far East was, most simply put, an enlargement of previously held properties. Britain rounded out her Indian Empire, and France did the same with her incipient Indochinese Empire. Even the new imperialist states intruding into this part of the world followed much the same process. The United States, or at least some of her more rabid citizens, had their eyes fixed on Hawaii well before the end of the century. Korea had already been invaded by Japan in the sixteenth century and continued to attract the attention of those seeking a place upon which the Japanese sun might shine. In Subsaharan Africa, where a supposed scramble had taken place, there really had not been any mad and undirected rush forward. France spread horizontally from Algeria, first eastward to Tunisia, then westward to Morocco. Britain spread vertically from the Cape Colony northward into East Central Africa and, later, from Egypt southward to the Sudan. In the heartland of Africa, a France moving from its littoral possessions gathered around the hump of West Africa clashed in its eastward drive with an England descending from the north. The point of intersection was Fashoda, and the moment of tension between the two imperialist nations has been called the Fashoda Incident of 1898.

There is no denying that the European newcomers picked up what they could where they could: Italy assumed a few favorable positions along the Red Sea coast; Leopold II of Belgium did quite handsomely with his enormous chunk of Central Africa; and Bismarckian Germany got a few pieces of the west and the east coasts of Africa and a few Pacific islands. This part of the grab was the least anticipated or foregone; yet even here the direction and limits of the expansion were largely conditioned by the positions and intentions of the two superimperialist powers, Great Britain and France.

The pegging out of empire was thus no completely haphazard effort. But the occupation and control of that empire was nonetheless very complicated and very perplexing. The new imperialism was new in the sense that it brought forth a wide range of ecological conditions and social problems to which all previous colonial experience was to contribute all too little by way of happy solutions. Although England had a continued and viable colonial tradition, her real expertise—and it was slow in being developed—was in the white, English-speaking dominions. Africa was initially an enigma. The other major colonial powers of the epoch were without meaningful tradition—the disastrous French policy in Algeria scarcely warranted imitation—and they were really starting *de nouveau*.

If imperialism is the disposition to expansion and its realization, empire is rule and administration. By the end of the nineteenth century the problems of empire loomed large. These problems derived, first, from particular colonial situations, and, second, from European attitudes toward these situations. Yet empire was always a two-way proposition: European attitudes toward the natives, native attitudes toward the Europeans.

Of the myriad of concerns and interests which soon confronted the European as colonial administrator, the first understood was that the new imperialism had transpired primarily in tropical climes in which large settlement colonies would be out of the question. Either the climate seemed initially to be unhealthy to the white man, or the teeming populations, as in Southeast Asia, allowed of little free space for new intruders. Moreover, the few serious attempts at colonization were not successful in numbers. Somewhat ironic to observe, the greatest era of European emigration had begun shortly before the age of imperialism, but that emigration was directed

primarily toward America. The new overseas possessions were to necessitate a new relationship between European administrator and local population. "Tropical dependencies" was the term used by the British to describe
many of these newly acquired regions; "dominations"
was the French phraseology of the time.

Whatever their affixed generic name, these new areas
were to be ruled—or better, administered—not populated, assimilated, or in any way incorporated into the
body politic of the metropolitan European state. On this
point almost all of the colonial experts agreed. The suggested relationship between colonial ruler and indigenous population might be described euphemistically as
an "association of two parties," but it was looked on more
rudely as a combination of European brains and native
muscle. Above all, the European function was to be directional. The analogy has been made between modern
overseas imperialism and medieval feudalism: the European colonial was to play the role of the lord of the
manor, while the natives played that of the serfs.

Theoretically, this asymmetrical relationship was justified primarily by the argument that the lands of the
world, regardless of present ownership, had to be
worked for the benefit of mankind. As one Frenchman
rationalized: "A race of men do not have the right to be
apart, to refuse all communication with others and to
leave their immense territories unused because they do
not know how to develop them." [5] And a Belgian later
added weight to these words: "On a vast continent,

[5] Albert Girault, *Principes de colonisation et de législation
coloniale* (Paris, 1894), p. 29.

nearly empty, some dozens of savages lived, lost in the immensity of the forests and the savannas, tolerated by a physical environment which they did not dominate, leading—as it were, on the edge of nature—a precarious existence. . . . The riches of the soil and the sub-soil were ignored, left to abandon, without master." The conclusion drawn from this statement is this: "The great colonial movement of the nineteenth century, the partition of Black Africa, is based not on the right of conquest, but on the right of occupation." [6] In brief, if a people does not know how to work its lands or does not care to, then another people with this knowledge and desire has the right of occupation.

The source of this particular attitude is pretty much derived from prevalent European economic attitudes. The same rationalization of economic activities—regulated labor, specialized functions, managerial direction —which so greatly accounts for European material superiority was found wanting in other parts of the world, a condition deemed disadvantageous. No less a person than Albert Schweitzer fully revealed the European bent of mind with respect to native labor in his *Edge of the Primeval Forest:*

The negro, then, under certain circumstances works well, but only so long as circumstances require it. The child of nature—here is the answer to the puzzle—is always a casual worker. In return for very little work nature supplies the native with nearly everything that he requires for his support in his village. . . . The negro, then, is not idle, but he

[6] Pierre Ryckmans, *Dominer pour servir* (Brussels, 1948), pp. 58–59.

is a free man. The wealth of the country cannot be exploited because the native has no interest in the process.

While Schweitzer's interpretation is not noticeably tainted with the racial concepts that are found in the writings of many imperialists of the time, his lines illustrate the ease with which the assumption of European superiority and native inferiority could be made. As Schweitzer also stated: "The negro is a child, and with children nothing can be done without the use of authority." At one with Schweitzer on this point, the imperialists were predisposed to consider their charges immediately incapable of or indifferent to responsible self-development. While Schweitzer restricted his comments to the Africa he thought he knew, such comments frequently appear regardless of the particular continent or people. In their new overseas possessions, the Europeans came to see themselves as indispensable guides, without whom the future would be repetitious of the past: economic stagnation, political anarchy, administrative corruption.

Airing such thoughts, the Europeans soon developed an imperial or colonial mentality, a sense of their own superiority, deriving not only from a superior material civilization but also from the belief in the superiority of their government, educational system, social customs, and the like. They created their own equivalent of manifest destiny, saw themselves as ruling races charged with civilizing missions, assumed they were tutors in the ways of the good life.

The obverse side of this easily assumed sense of European superiority was a similar but enforced sense of native inferiority. The local populations, where they came into contact with the European, were made to see that their customs and institutions were not comparable to those of their conquerors. Nehru bitterly commented on this in *Toward Freedom:*

We developed the mentality of good country-house servants. Sometimes we were treated to a rare honor—we were given a cup of tea in the drawing room. The height of our ambition was to become respectable and to be promoted individually to the upper regions. Greater than any victory of arms or diplomacy was this psychological triumph of the British in India.

Several social and psychological theories about the "colonial situation," the confrontation of European and native, have been erected.[7] But no author to date has presented the problem more provocatively than Albert Memmi, a North African novelist, whose assessment of colonialism is often very revealing. It is his thesis that both "colonialist" and "colonized" have to be created, that prior to the advent of colonial rule there is no predisposition of one or the other to assume his particular role.

There is only a particle of truth in the fashionable notion of "dependency complex" and "colonizability," etc. There undoubtedly exists—at some point in its evolution—a certain adherence of the colonized to colonization. However, this adherence is the result of colonization not its cause. It arises

[7] See, for instance, Albert Mannoni, *Psychologie de la colonisation* (Paris, 1950), and Georges Balandier, *Sociologie actuelle de l'Afrique noire* (Paris, 1955), Chapter 1.

after and not before colonial occupation. In order for the colonizer to be complete master, it is not enough for him to be so in actual fact, but he must also believe in its legitimacy. In order for the legitimacy to be complete, it is not enough for the colonized to be a slave, he must also accept his role. The bond between the colonizer and the colonized is thus destructive and creative. It destroys and re-creates the two partners of colonization into colonizer and colonized.[8]

Whether it is, as Memmi asserts, that the colonizer must legitimize his initial usurpation in order to be able to live with himself, it is patently clear that a paternalistic attitude at best and a contemptuous attitude at worst developed within the European colonial mind and led to little social or intellectual intercourse between colonizer and colonized. No more striking description of the effects of this attitude is to be found than that of the "bridge party" which takes place in E. M. Forster's *Passage to India.* To accommodate the desires of some newly arrived Englishwomen an official's wife arranges a lawn party to bridge the gap between Hindu and Anglo-Indian. But the party is not a success, as the Anglo-Indians remain haughtily on the higher portion of the lawn while the Hindus hesitatingly stand together on the lower portion. There is no "bridge party" at all. Rather, as Kipling put it earlier, "Never the twain shall meet."

Two communities came to exist in almost every colonial region: the small but dominant European nucleus and the indigenous mass. Juxtaposed they were, but certainly seldom socially interrelated. Even the traditionally

[8] Albert Memmi, *The Colonizer and the Colonized* (New York, 1965), pp. 88–89.

nonracial French could, on occasion, find reason for social separation of the races. Speaking of urbanism in Dakar, Senegal, Charles Morazé wrote in 1936:

Formerly Europeans and natives lived mixed together. Innumerable families were heaped together in small rooms, true caravansaries blended together in the European town. This promiscuity was deplorable. Europeans and natives were not subject to the same epidemics; yellow fever, for example, mortal for the white, is benign in the negro. The danger of a mixed population was that epidemics were able to spread without being quickly checked. Finally, the system lacked elegance. Thus, in 1916 it was decided to create the native village of the medina.[9]

The polar extremes which the Europeans thus fixed for themselves and their charges further led to the assumption that colonial rule would of necessity be of long duration. From their comfortable heights many nineteenth-century theorists asserted that the colonial territories would of course eventually become independent, but "eventually" was usually conceived of as meaning many decades, perhaps centuries. Paul Leroy-Beaulieu, the French colonial expert, was sure some three hundred years would be necessary before most of France's new possessions would be ready to handle their own affairs. Even between the two world wars the clearest feature of British colonial policy was "the tranquil assumption of the long-term character of colonial rule."[10]

[9] Charles Morazé, "Dakar," *Annales de géographie* (March 15, 1936), p. 360.
[10] Kenneth Robinson, *The Dilemmas of Trusteeship* (London, 1965), p. 7.

What the new imperialists had done was to create their own political dilemma: the continued necessity of their political domination, yet the suggestion of eventual colonial independence. No one better presented this dilemma than did the Earl of Cromer, who stated that the Englishman, in considering imperial objectives ". . . is in truth always striving to attain two ideals, which are mutually destructive—the ideal of good government, which connotes the continuance of his own superiority, and the ideal of self-government, which connotes the whole or partial abdication of his own supreme position." Condescending toward the native populations, the European imperialists and colonial administrators complacently and imperiously assumed the "white man's burden," the "tutelage of the lesser breeds." But, as is well known, nothing is less easily parted with than self-righteousness. As late as the 1950's the Belgians were still speaking of a sacred civilizing mission.[11]

Finally, this prevalent attitude led to something of a self-fulfilling prophecy. Believing that native retardedness was a reality and that colonial rule would endure, the Europeans did all too little toward the preparation of their possessions for eventual self-rule. While the British come out better than most other colonials on this score, their over-all record is not an exceptionally inspiring one. Lord Bryce, viewing India at the end of the nineteenth century, offered this pertinent comment: "The government of India by the English resembles that of her provinces by Rome in being virtually despotic. In both cases,

[11] See Belgian Government Information Service, *The Sacred Mission of Civilization* (New York, 1953).

whatever may have been done for the people, nothing is done by the people."

In brief, the colonized peoples were nowhere seriously asked to participate in the decision-making or policy formulation taking place in their own lands. They were directed and guided, often by gentle and well-meaning hands, but they were not allowed to tamper with the administrative machinery. We now know that the European imperialists and colonial administrators who arrived at these conclusions were generally self-deluding. And yet perhaps they had reason to be.

In those rather halcyon days before World War I imperialist policy was not without its appeal to certain elements within the native populations. Once the task of pacifying the area over which the European flags flew had been achieved, the acceptance or acquiescence in colonial rule was rather widespread. The resentment and national fervor which were later to rend apart colonial empires were nowhere in prominent evidence in the new possessions. This is not to say that nationalism did not exist anywhere outside of the West. Interestingly enough, its first far-off reverberations were in old empires: Manchu China with the Revolution of 1911, the Spanish Empire with the uprising of the Philippines, Japan with the Meiji Era, and even the British Empire with Canada's demands for autonomy. If, however, nationalism seemed to appear in incipient form in places such as India and Indochina before World War I, neither European nor native seriously entertained any thoughts about early independence. As Nehru said, to become respectable was still the height of general native ambition. Those few initiated into the ways of the West, either by European education or its colonial facsimile, aspired to be part of this new order. In the French colonies of West Africa they became the *évolués*, those persons brought up sufficiently to Western standards to act as negotiators between ruling minority and dominated mass. And others, less well placed but supposedly blessed with a smattering of the ruler's language and customs, like Joyce Carey's hero in *Mister Johnson*, did all they could to please, even if they could not fully understand.

In this respect Albert Memmi is quite correct: the colonized were created, usually forced to accept a new and inferior status, although on occasion they fell into that status when the European, like Albert Schweitzer, exercised a benign philanthropy. But this statement is something of an anticipation, for the striking feature of the new imperialism in its initial stage was that it really affected no great numbers of natives or Europeans. Just as the European taxpayer could afford imperialism because it was not too expensive a luxury, so the average native could ignore the phenomenon, so remote was it from his daily existence. Would it be presumptuous to suggest as a generalization the following: the seeming initial success of modern imperialism was the result of the ignorance of colonizer and colonized of what imperialism really meant or was to mean?

From the above analysis it might appear that the first and second phases of European overseas expansion were more characterized by their similarities than by their differences. Proclaimed economic needs combined with power politics brought certain portions of the world under European control in the first period, and nearly all of the remaining regions under European control in the second. As was stated at the beginning of this study, causal factors offer little variety even when viewed across the centuries. The trilogy of God, gold, and glory remains a handy way of summing up the entire enterprise.

This much said, there are some other points which should be considered. If causes remain consistent, methods and abilities had changed. First, the older agency of the chartered company as spearhead of the imperialist endeavor had declined. There were, of course, many concessionary companies existing in the first days of the new wave of imperialism, as the Royal Niger Company or Rhodes' South Africa Company indicate. French exploitation of Equatorial Africa and Belgian exploitation of the Congo were ruthlessly initiated by such companies. Nonetheless, their role was far more short-lived and insignificant than that of their predecessors. Their greatest success was in Subsaharan Africa, but elsewhere more direct state control was initiated, and even in Subsaharan Africa the concessionary company was replaced nearly everywhere within the first three decades of the new imperialism. Second, the degree of European success—the ability to lord it over alien populations, the ability to amass huge empires grossly disproportionate to the size of the colonial nation—was very much greater in the nineteenth century than in the sixteenth. The power that made this possible was essentially industrial, and the industries of the new Europe required raw materials from all over the world to feed them. In contrast to the Europe of Queen Elizabeth I and Louis XIV, that of Gladstone and Bismarck was economically very advanced. Domination of the world's trade and resources now became a European objective. But, in truth, empire was less the source of financial investment or the outlet for goods than it was the source of raw materials. Rubber, oil, tin, cocoa, peanuts, and phosphates are all part of the long bill of lading which Europe compiled.

Along with this newfound industrial and political power—indeed, a part of it—was the nationalist fervor with which imperialism was engaged. Although never winning over the majority of the articulate European population, imperialism was nonetheless popular, as is exemplified by the *Kolonial Gesellschaft* of Germany with its 100,000 membership at the turn of the century. Similar organizations existed in other countries, with even the Fabians in England providing a deferential nod in the direction of empire.[12] The prestige of empire was never higher, nor was its power.

Finally, the new imperialism was soon accompanied by a new attitude of responsibility and obligation. We contemporaries probably find this attitude maudlin, and we imagine it to have been often as much pose as sincere intention. But regardless of our appraisal of it, many late-nineteenth-century Europeans convinced themselves that they were discharging a significant burden by helping the "lesser breeds." The condescension, the phlegmatic

---

[12] On this subject see Bernard Semmel, *Imperialism and Social Reform, English Imperial Thought, 1895–1914* (Cambridge, Mass.), 1960.

aloofness with which they carried forth this burden is certainly reproachable, but the point remains that, unlike their earlier imperialist predecessors, they set about working out a "native policy," a suitable rapport between colonizer and colonized. What is most significant in this attitude was its clear-cut implication of responsibility, and this, in turn, meant the injection of moral issues. Perhaps the very acknowledgment of the matter of morality in imperialism made the late nineteenth-century European effort all the more incongruous, if not grotesque, but with the twentieth century genuine attempts at reform were made, and imperialism began to undergo a transition which was ultimately to lead to its own elimination.

4 . EMPIRES IN TRANSITION

The winds of change, which Prime Minister Macmillan was to sense many years later, were already blowing across the colonial domains in the interwar period. Their direction, however, was not easily determined. Did they come out of the East or out of the West? Were the changes in colonial administration principally the result of the demands and opposition of imperialized peoples like the Indians, Indochinese, and Indonesians; or were they principally the result of new policies initiated by the colonial powers themselves? These are old questions, and they have been answered many times—with intention being confused with accident, with concession being called capitulation, and, of course, with virtue being made of necessity.

This much can be easily granted: in these years of transition, colonial nationalism was beginning to rise as a force in most of the European empires; and in these years of transition colonial administrators and home governments were seriously grappling with the many colonial problems they now encountered. The interaction of these two developments induced the transformation of imperialism: the movement from colonial domination to colonial devolution was thus begun, but its outcome was still far from determined.

The rise of colonial nationalism is a story often and well told, as it should be, for this form of nationalism grew in significance as it grew in strength from the end of World War I until the present.[1] While its greatest importance was registered in the decade of 1950, its major constituent elements were in place before then: Wilsonian ideals about self-determination, Leninist ideas about capitalistic colonial exploitation, older European liberal and democratic ideas coming from seventeenth-century English contractual thought and eighteenth-century French revolutionary thought. In almost every colonial domain articulate leaders, now quite knowledgeable in the ways of the West, were to employ European ideas and principles to demand a greater role in the government of their own country. Some among them even

---

[1] See particularly, Rupert Emerson, *From Empire to Nation* (Boston, 1962); and Thomas Hodgkin, *Nationalism in Colonial Africa* (New York, 1957).

went further and demanded what the Europeans never clearly promised them: the right to determine completely their own political fates.

These men operated in no intellectual vacuum, for they were already provided with some telling examples to follow. The modernization of Japan, historically marked by the successful outcome of the Russo-Japanese War of 1904–1905, had its impact on the East, where Japan was now viewed as proof of Asiatic ability to adapt and Asiatic ability to repel the white man. In a lesser way the Chinese Revolution of 1911, which ended the inept Manchu rule and which ushered in a republican form of government, also had its impact. Across the continent in Turkey, Mustapha Kemal created a modern and efficient national state almost phoenix-like out of the ashes of the old Ottoman Empire. And, perhaps most significant of all, the advent of the Communists to power in Russia provided new hope and inspiration—and, much later, aid—to more than one country in the colonial world. Old empires and segments of them demonstrated their ability to reform and reshape their political institutions and, hence, their political destinies.

Of all the attempts at colonial change in this interwar period, none is more significant than that of India. Before any of the other colonial regions strongly felt the initial gusts of the winds of nationalism, India had already been swept.

The direction toward colonial reform in British India was given before the interwar period had fully opened. Such measures as those bearing the names Morley-Minto

(1909) and Montagu-Chelmsford (1919) began the process of representative government, while the British recognition in 1917 of Indian dominion status and the right of eventual self-rule patterned future Anglo-Indian relations. Yet there was considerable friction in the decade of the 1930's, friction resulting from the Indian political movement forward and the English attempt to brake it. One author has assessed this action in a different and interesting way. He contends that "with Indians demanding political rights and the British conceding ultimate self-government . . . what was left to fight about? In the ultimate sense there was very little." [2] Of course, the key word is the adjective "ultimate." The Indian nationalists, in their wisdom, believed that the value of continued British rule was negligible. The English, in their wisdom, believed that the value of their continued rule was considerable. Each party knew that the other was proceeding in the same direction, but here, as in most later colonial situations, we are faced with the problem of timing: the speed so often demanded by the colonial people, the slowness desired by the colonial power.

The devolution of empire, which the political process in India clearly indicated, was one in which the real initiative lay with the native population—in this instance, Gandhi's Congress Party. Founded as far back as 1885, Congress became a nationalist movement before it was a contending political party. Essentially a creation of the

[2] Percival Spear, *India: A Modern History* (Ann Arbor, 1961), p. 343.

English-trained professional classes, Congress broadened its base in the interwar years, thanks to the efforts of Gandhi, who was able to identify with the Indian people in a way that few leaders could. Congress now came to represent the several masses of India—notably Hindu and Moslem—and to be the driving force toward the objective of *swaraj*, self-rule.

The success of Congress was, however, equally dependent upon the British attitude. Even the bitterest critics of British colonial policy do concede that much intelligence and political insight were revealed during this period. British resistance to Indian nationalism was seldom truly obstinate and often enlightened. The empirical British played the game by ear; as a result they recognized the rumblings of nationalism.

Elsewhere around the globe there were rumblings which attracted attention and forewarned of graver events yet ahead. Scarcely had World War I ended, when on November 13, 1918, Sa'd Zaghlul Pasha, an able and ambitious politician, requested of the British representative in Egypt the right to go to England to demand the independence of Egypt. His request was refused, but the delegation he headed in Egypt and which he claimed represented the Egyptian nation grew into the Wafd (delegation) Party and entrained Egyptian nationalism between the wars. At the southern tip of Africa, nationalism also appeared in rather bitter form as the Nationalist Party under the leadership of General Hertzog attempted to wrest control of the government from the British in the Union of South Africa. This party introduced the principle of *apartheid* which, several decades later, was to become official policy and was to aggravate African politics.

In Southeast Asia nationalism was already reaching large proportions. In Indonesia the foundation of the religious-nationalist movement, Sarekat Islam, dated from 1911, but its importance really dates from the postwar era. Even then, however, it was to be challenged by the Indonesian Communist Party, which was sufficiently well organized and militant to create an uprising in 1926–1927 which harassed the Dutch. From Indochina similar signs of discontent were discernible. Again, nationalist organizations existed before the war, but it was the large numbers of returning veterans who swelled the nationalist movement and enlarged it into an important French problem. Splintered as it was, Indochinese nationalism took on no uniform shape, but its outstanding leader, Ho Chi Minh, and its outstanding doctrine were essentially Communist. Again, as in Indonesia, an outburst of Communist terror occurred, this time in 1929.

There were also lesser noises which perhaps should have attracted more attention at the time than they did. Garveyism, something of a forerunner of Pan-Africanism, spread from the United States, where it was founded, to Africa, where it was intended, and intimated at future nationalism in its doctrine of "Africa for the Africans." The West African Students' Union, which was created in 1925 as a residence for Africans in London, soon became a forum of African discontent and later "graduated" some important African nationalists, of whom

Kwame Nkrumah is the most famous. Even from the West Indies in the late 1930's came news of uprisings in Trinidad and Jamaica, which may not be easily labeled "nationalist," but which were clear indications of dissatisfaction with British rule there.

While the examples of colonial nationalist activities in the interwar period may not be legion, they are of sufficient number and importance to suggest that in some parts of the world the old colonial order was being challenged.

So far we have been treating nationalism rather metaphorically, as a meteorological phenomenon: a wind or a storm. But if these terms best describe it as a force, they provide little understanding of the component elements of that force. What one must know is something about the people who helped generate this colonial nationalism.

To begin with a sweeping but not inappropriate generalization, we can say that they were part of a new elite which rose in response to the colonial presence. What the juxtaposition of European and native civilizations invariably resulted in was social change. Not that the Europeans ever consciously worked for the overthrow or the serious modification of the pre-existing social order. Except for the minimum of changes desirable and necessary for successful rule, they retained what they found and built upon it, for they realized that their control could best be structured on local institutions and maintained through the cooperation of local leaders. To be crude, they used what they found. But they also represented another civilization, another political and social order

which stood in opposition to the local one, which dominated it, and, which by its very existence, suggested the
inadequacies and weaknesses of the other.

The response to this new condition of things was culturally as well as socially jarring. Some groups sought to
incorporate much of the new into the old, to work the
most glaring and intrusive aspects of the newly arrived
culture into the old cultural pattern as a means of de-
fending it. Others openly rebelled. But for the most
educated and radical-minded of the younger generation
who were exposed most directly and frequently to the
local aspects of European civilization, change in the
sense of radical adaptation seemed the chief hope for
their society and country. These were to become marginal men who placed themselves on the periphery of their
own society by their personal initiation into the ways of
the West and by their inability to gain full acceptance
into the foreign ruling circle. They were the first generation of that intellectual and politically active elite who
were later to lead their countries to independence.

Lest the impression be given, however, that these colonial elites were created *ex nihilo*, it would be advisable
to draw the reader's attention to their social origins.
While questioning their own society and deviating from
its forms, they usually came from the "right families."
They did not appear in random fashion, but emerged
from the already dominant social and economic levels of
autochthonous society.[3] They were those persons who
could afford the luxury of a European education, who

[3] On this subject see Fatma Mansur, *Process of Independence*
(London, 1963), notably p. 65.

enjoyed sufficient social mobility to enter the new professions, such as law or foreign commerce, who were able to constitute a new bourgeoisie whose strength rested less on money than on position. In sum, few were those among this first generation who rose, Horatio Alger-like, from humble origins.

Initially, the general direction of these elites was not toward immediate national independence but toward the politization of imperial rule. They wished to convert the colonial administrative system into a political system, one in which they would have a voice, a vote, an office to fill. If anything, representative government and constitutional forms became their immediate objectives, derived, of course, from the European precedent. Speaking the language and understanding the thought of their conquerors, they used the argument, the principles, and the methods of nineteenth-century Europe to their own advantage. They wrote tracts, founded newspapers, held rallies, formed clubs, and began political parties.

If encapsulated, the history of these new colonial elites through the interwar years would read more as one of qualified acceptance of foreign rule than as one of intransigent opposition to it. True, there was already an advanced guard of militant nationalists which included men like Nguyen Ai Quoc (the future Ho Chi Minh) of Indochina, Mahatma Gandhi of India, and Mohammed Hatta of Indonesia. But the majority were by and large more moderate or less advanced than this. Or perhaps they were more pessimistic, acutely aware of the still preponderant power which the colonial administrators could and did bring to bear. Whatever the reasons, they chose to make cooperation the policy to follow, but that form of cooperation which would assure themselves more authority, more power.

To be sure, the process of nationalism was not one which can be graphed with a curve sweeping gracefully upward. The line of development was frequently interrupted or altered by bulky obstacles: the recalcitrance of the imperialists to alter the status quo they had established; the animosities and rivalries of tribes and cultural groupings within the colonial unit; the lethargy and ignorance of the mass of the population who remained illiterate and politically uninitiated.

All of this suggests that any general evaluation of colonial nationalism at this stage of development must be qualified. That it was beginning and gaining momentum in these years is certain, but its progress was erratic, varying from region to region, even colony to colony. If reaching the level of irresistibility in a few places such as India, it was not noticeable in many others, such as French West Africa. Only after World War II, when the imperialist will and wherewithal were greatly impaired and when a semblance of popular support was attached to it, did nationalism sweep in one great arc through the colonial world, from India to Tunisia and on to Guinea. Then its leadership was frequently that of angry young men who were not given to compromise or discussion of legal niceties. Like Nkrumah they exclaimed, "Self-government now!" Like Tom Mboya they sneered, "Europeans, scram out of Africa!"

The danger of overemphasizing the immediate effects of the first winds of nationalism should now be apparent.

In retrospect we see what they have done; we know that they were to sweep colonial empires away. But in the interwar years these winds were still not irresistible in most places and were frequently not very formidable. The European colonial powers could and still did respond with sufficient force to contain them.

When viewed from above or from far away as by colonial administrator or by home government, empires did not appear to be in a state of hopeless disrepair. On the contrary, about all that seemed necessary to keep them in good order were a few institutional modifications, a few altered attitudes. As the colonial administrators saw it, imperialism was entering a new phase: that of responsible empire, of constructive economic and social development, of cooperation between ruler and ruled. In the rather pretentious words uttered by the former French Minister of Colonies, Albert Sarraut, in 1923:

The hour has come for a general and precise method of action in place of isolated and uncertain efforts. This can be done all the better now that the period of territorial enlargement is closed for our overseas domain. Henceforth relieved of the obligations of conquest, French labor in the colonies can be entirely consecrated to the organization of the full development of its patrimony.[4]

This *mise en valeur*, the economic and social development of the colonial possessions, was everywhere viewed as the next and more noble task confronting the imperialist nations. The sanguine hope was that the indigenous

[4] Albert Sarraut, *La Mise en valeur des colonies françaises* (Paris, 1923), pp. 25–26.

populations would follow the ways of the European or, at least, his advice. Speaking of Algeria in 1928, a high-placed French official could happily announce: "We have the good fortune to see this native elite, through its excellent frame of mind, decide to walk along our own road, for, educated by us, it has an appreciation of the French method and of French thought."[5] He was not far wrong, for as late as 1936, Ferhat Abbas, later an important leader in the Algerian nationalist movement, was to write a pamphlet expounding and praising the idea of *French* Algeria.

So, in an atmosphere that still seemed relatively tranquil to them, Europeans turned to the problems of colonial evolution, problems which they still intended to solve themselves.

The transformation of imperialism into something resembling responsible empire did not happen suddenly or unattended. Many intimations preceded the important discussions of the interwar era. Throughout the history of European overseas expansion there were moments and occasions when pleas for respect of native institutions, or demands for autonomous rule, or requests for assistance to backward peoples were made. Dominicans, Jesuits, Quakers, and Enlightenment philosophers all so expressed themselves in the sixteenth, seventeenth, and

[5] Speech delivered by Jean Melia, former French High Commissioner in Syria and *Chef du Cabinet* of the Governor General of Algeria, on November 19, 1928, before the Comité d'Etudes sociales et politiques de Genève. Reprinted in *L'Etat d'esprit actuel des indigènes dans les colonies des différents pays* (Geneva, 1928), pp. 22–23.

eighteenth centuries. Examples are easily found. Las Casas posited as a principle the thought that the American Indians "should be governed for their own spiritual and temporal well-being." The so-called Clapham Sect, led by dedicated men like Thomas Clarkson and William Wilberforce, aroused late-eighteenth-century English public opinion against the inequities of the slave trade. And Rousseau's statement that man is born free but everywhere is in chains could be and was interpreted to mean that the civilization of the West was no better than any other, that respect for all cultures was merited.

But the most famous argument to come out of that age was the one presented by Edmund Burke in his 1783 speech in defense of Pitt's East India Bill. Speaking of the East India Company's power and authority, Burke commented:

. . . such rights, or privileges, or whatever else you choose to call them, are in the very strictest sense a *trust:* and it is of the very essence of every *trust* to be rendered accountable. . . .

Here is the trust idea first well-expounded as a governing principle, the idea which the British were to make famous and their own standard for empire in the twentieth century. By the time the new wave of imperialism surged forth certain concepts of European responsibility and accountability toward colonial peoples were actually defined. Beyond the polemics over the "white man's burden" and the "civilizing mission" were often found sincere thoughts. The Europeans believed that they had assumed a moral obligation when they incurred the responsibility of empire. Perhaps it was the result of pangs of conscience, as Albert Schweitzer believed.

We and our civilization are burdened, really with a great debt. We are not free to confer benefits on these men, or not, as we please; it is our duty. Anything we give them is not benevolence but atonement.[6]

And perhaps it was the result of great pride, of ethnocentric enthusiasm for the civilization the imperialists cherished and believed so superior. To confer on other peoples the benefits of modern Europe was viewed as a noble endeavor.

Whatever and however sincere the motives, the professed desire to "civilize" took on popular proportions even before the end of World War I, although the manner of its implementation was more often than not vague. At the Berlin West African Conference, held in the winter of 1884–1885, the tone was publicly set, the objective diplomatically subscribed to.

All the Powers exercising sovereign rights, or having influence in the said territories, undertake to watch over the preservation of the native races, and the amelioration of the moral and material conditions of their existence.

Such was the wording of the General Act of the Conference, an act to which representatives of most of the nations of Europe—and all of the colonial powers—willingly affixed their signatures.

Between 1885 and the end of World War I a number

[6] Schweitzer, *op. cit.*, p. 115.

of authors enlarged upon the idea contained in the General Act by insisting upon the international responsibility, the accountability of the imperialist powers to all of civilization. J. A. Hobson, Theodore Roosevelt, and Walter Lippmann, to name some of the more distinguished, contributed to this body of literature. Even the arch advocate of British Empire, the Colonial Secretary, Joseph Chamberlain, recognized the moral burden incumbent upon his nation. "We feel now that our rule over these territories [those in the tropics] can only be justified if we can show that it adds to the happiness and prosperity of the people," he declared in a speech of March 31, 1897. From the narrower confines of national satisfaction to the broader vistas of international service the argument over the *raison d'être* of empire slowly moved, reaching an important stage of development immediately after World War I.

World War I certainly did not have the impact on imperialist affairs that World War II did. Military activities and peace settlements were primarily European-centered with the rest of the world on the periphery of it all. Nonetheless, colonial affairs did intrude and were introduced. Many political leaders acknowledged their country's indebtedness to the colonies for their effort in the war—note only the number of troops supplied by British India or French West Africa—and many critics felt the shattering impact of the war on the earlier easy confidence in the superiority of European civilization. But these factors weighed less than the discussions and principles upon which the colonies of the defeated German Empire were to be treated. The Peace Conference at

Versailles witnessed the birth of the mandate system. Much has been said and written about the mandate system. In the opinion of some commentators it was a flimsy device with which to screen the furtherance of the imperialism of the victorious powers. In the opinion of others it was a major step toward the realization of the idea of international political responsibility, of trusteeship. Without hedging, we can say that it was both.

By the secret Sikes-Picot treaty of 1916 Great Britain and France had intended to serve their imperial purposes by segmenting the Ottoman Empire into spheres of influence. This early decision, however, could hardly be squared with the Fourteen Points President Wilson enunciated late in the war, which struck out against annexations and secret treaties, and which became the basis for armistice negotiations. In the corridors of Versailles a compromise was sought between European *Realpolitik* and Wilsonian idealism. The outcome was the mandate idea, the charging of certain states with the responsibility of administering the former territories of the Ottoman and German Empires without acquiring *de jure* sovereignty over them. However, the real effect did have many of the marks of the old imperialism. Rather than place these territories under a "neutral" mandatory, such as Denmark or Sweden, as some people had suggested, the victors at Versailles assigned them to the outstanding colonial powers: Great Britain, France, Japan, and Belgium. Moreover, the strong demands of the Union of South Africa for control of former German Southwest Africa and of Australia and New Zealand for some of the German Pacific islands were recognized, thus allowing a form of local imperialism to be carried on. In addition, the later history of the mandatory powers also reveals that administrative devices were used to bring the mandated territories within the colonial sphere. For instance, France allied certain services in Togo with those in her colony of Dahomey, and Belgium joined Ruanda-Urundi to the Congo administratively.

Nevertheless, the attention given to the idea of trust, of international responsibility on the part of the mandatory power over the mandated territory, was surely a sincere reiteration and elaboration of words written at the West African Conference. Article 22 of the Covenant of the League of Nations contained the thought, and the first two paragraphs of that article set the standard:

To those colonies and territories which as a consequence of the late war have ceased to be under sovereignty of the States which formerly governed them, and which are inhabited by peoples not yet able to stand by themselves under the strenuous conditions of the modern world, there should be applied the principle that the well-being and development of such peoples form a sacred trust of civilization. . . .

The best method of giving practical effect to this principle is that the tutelage of such peoples should be entrusted to advanced nations, who, by reason of their resources, experience, or their geographical position, can best undertake this responsibility. . . .

The phrasing is high-flown, but what does it mean historically? Lord Lugard, the architect of the Nigerian political system and one of Britain's truly outstanding colonial administrators, thought it meant a great deal. "The Mandate system is a new departure in international law

93

and policy, in that it confers sovereignty under definite obligations, for the fulfilment of which the Mandatory is responsible to a constituted authority." [7] That particular authority, of course, was the League of Nations or more exactly the Permanent Mandates Commission, which was to receive reports from the mandatories and review their actions. Unlike earlier types of mandates, the most famous being that "given" Leopold II over the Congo by the Berlin Conference, the League system provided for an international organization which was supposed to observe the mandatory's work with an eye clearly fixed on native interests, on responsible trusteeship. If this was a new departure in principle, there was no comparable new departure in practice. Effective international control was never achieved as the League lacked the necessary authority, so that whatever obligation to the ideals of trusteeship was felt by the mandatory powers came chiefly from within, not without.

Perhaps the lasting result of the debate over mandates was not the machinery but the mood which developed out of it. Henceforth particular national interests occupied only a portion of the thought and concern of the colonial thinkers and high administrators; the rest was occupied by the broader ethical implications, by a supranational responsibility. In Lugard's now famous phrase the Dual Mandate had come into existence.

The Dual Mandate was moral and material: first, the "civilizing mission," the realization of the "sacred trust"

[7] Lord Lugard, *The Dual Mandate* (London, 1965), p. 53. This new edition contains a valuable introduction by Margery Perham, Lugard's biographer.

given to the more advanced nations; second, the "open door," the opening of the colonial regions to the economies of the world, along with their material development for the benefit of the local populations.

Lugard thus combined the two dominant themes which had been woven into the pattern of modern imperialism but gave them a stronger ethical basis. His own words provide the moral tone:

> The responsibility is one which the advantages of an inherited civilization and a superior intellectual culture, no less than the physical superiority conferred by monopoly of firearms, imposes upon the controlling power. To the backward races civilisation must be made to mean something higher than the aims and methods of the development syndicate or the assiduous cultivation of new wants. Where these principles have been neglected, history has taught us that failure has been the result.[8]

Lugard could pride himself on the fact that the Dual Mandate was essentially a British policy with a British past, but the idea had reverberations elsewhere. Across the Channel Albert Sarraut paralleled Lugard's thought in his influential study *La Mise en valeur des colonies françaises*. "France," he proclaimed, "is going to organize the development of the territories and resources of these backward colonies . . . to her own advantage no doubt, *but also to the general advantage of the world*." Again in concord with Lugard, he acknowledged the "moral superiority" of certain nations over other races: "this other idea of the obligation of fair and just tutelage

[8] *Ibid.*, p. 58.

which is the legitimate basis of the sovereignty or protectorate established by these nations over those races."

The trust idea and Dual Mandate, which was widely subscribed to between the wars, has had its share of criticism.[9] It still smacked of excessive paternalism, of the we-know-best attitude with which European imperialism had been morally justified at least since the time when Livingstone sought to bring the principles of Christianity and free trade into East Africa. It supposed, but did not prescribe sufficiently for its realization, a cooperative European-native effort to bring the colonial regions quickly and surely onto the European economic scene despite the vast disparity in their contemporary stages of development. It never clearly defined the objective of self-government or the manner in which it might be attained, yet its moralistic overtones about "sacred trust" certainly implied evolution in that direction. In brief the Dual Mandate might be considered but another variation on a fifty-year-old theme.

Such consideration would be unfair. Although the Dual Mandate idea was vague in its implications, it did depend upon a change of attitude in colonial affairs that was genuine. In place of domination, or of unidirectional assimilation, or of crude exploitation, cooperation and responsibility were the principles evoked and believed in.

The sources of this new and prevalent colonial attitude are varied. First, the science of anthropology had at last been weaned from a mischievous Social Darwinism

[9] The ideas here presented derive principally from Kenneth Robinson, *The Dilemmas of Trusteeship* (Oxford, 1962); and Duncan Hall, *Mandates, Dependencies and Trusteeship* (Washington, 1948.)

and moved to a mature phase of development through the study of comparative cultures. Men like Malinowski, Radcliffe-Brown, Evans-Pritchard, and Lévy-Bruhl turned their attention to Polynesian and African cultures and published works which awakened the colonial administrator and the government official to the need for a more circumspect policy, one recognizing cultural differences. Within narrower colonial circles, such methodical approaches had already been introduced. For instance, the French administrator and teacher Maurice Delafosse published a serious study of Negro cultures in 1922, and Lord Lugard suggested the need for careful anthropological studies upon which the colonial administrator could base his policy. Toward the end of the interwar period, the French government established its Institut français d'Afrique noire, which, placed within the African colonies, became a base for careful field studies. As a result of all this intellectual activity a growing appreciation of cultural variations and of the integrity of cultural systems was developed in Europe. Margery Perham, the English colonial historian and friend of Lord Lugard, summed up this attitude when she wrote in 1934: "A growing knowledge of African society has taught us a new respect for it."

Second, a growing amount of criticism of imperialism was having its impact on colonial thought and practice. The interwar period witnessed a considerable amount of political agitation against imperialism. In Britain, elements within the Labour Party spoke out forcefully for some form of internationalization of all empires, such as provided for in the mandate system. In France, the

French Socialist Party demanded a more humanistic colonial policy, one in which France would really assume the role of guide and responsible guardian. Furthermore, such public manifestations as the Brussels Congress Against Imperialism and Colonial Oppression of February 1927, at which men like Nehru of India and Mohammed Hatta of Indonesia spoke, forced attention on the colonial problem. Then there were a welter of publications on the theme "Do Colonies Pay?" and a handful of trenchant personal revelations, like André Gide's *Voyage to the Congo*, which raised doubts about the value and purposes of imperialism.

Third, a new generation of colonial administrators were now beating the bush. Perhaps the motives of their Victorian predecessors were every bit as high as theirs, but this new group tended to be more observant, more considerate, more alert to and interested in local colonial problems. For instance, the District Commissioners ("D.C.'s") of the British African colonies soon became justly praised and continued to be, as the commentary of John Gunther in *Inside Africa* indicates.

Not only did these factors affect colonial attitudes but they also heightened the enthusiasm for a colonial practice which had made its appearance before World War I but which was now to be more widely applied and was to be celebrated as theory. This was indirect rule. If the Dutch, Belgians, English, and French all could claim some authorship of this practice, the credit for its development belongs chiefly to Lord Lugard.

Indirect rule was an *ad hoc* arrangement which Lugard first practiced in Northern Nigeria and to which he later appended a theory. What Lugard did was simply to recognize some obvious facts and then work with them. He initially lacked the necessary trained personnel with which to administer his Northern Territory effectively. In this region, however, Fulani control over Hausaland was still quite effective. Realizing this, Lugard continued the pre-existing system, leaving to the emirs their established political positions. The few English political officers were to work with and through the emirs, but not over them. Lugard wanted his English personnel to be as inconspicuous as possible. The system seemed to work; it was a cheap form of administration—Lugard never denied this—and it was praised as a just and undisruptive form of colonial administration.

Although Lugard's own *Political Memoranda* spell out the policy at great length, one of the most coherent and favorable defenses of indirect rule was made by Margery Perham in 1934. While Miss Perham granted that indirect rule was an example of necessity becoming a virtue, she also insisted that such rule was consonant with native abilities and with the growing European appreciation of cultural relativism. The chief glory of indirect rule was its acceptance of indigenous institutions, acceptance with the purpose of incorporating them into a single governmental system, all the while they were subjected "to the continuous guidance, supervision, and stimulus of European officers." "The great task of indirect rule is to hold the ring, to preserve a fair field within which Africans can strike their own balance between conservatism and adaptation." Not designed to result in social stasis, indirect rule was to be a flexible, *ad hoc* working arrangement between two cultures now met. As such it was a transitional method, and "the immediate test of its success will be the frequency with which it receives and requires revision in response to progress." [10] While the British exercised their new policy with varying degrees of success in Africa from Nigeria in the west to Tanganyika in the east, other colonial administrations in other empires engaged in somewhat similar practices. The Dutch, for instance, prided themselves on their empirical policy in Indonesia. One of their outstanding colonial theorists wrote, "The Dutch regime is inspired in practice by the spirit of indirect government much more than the theory might indicate." [11] The Controllers in the various Exterior Territories—those lying outside of Java—resembled Lugard's Political Officers in Nigeria, with one notable exception. While Lugard insisted that his Political Officers at no time directly intrude in local affairs, the Dutch Controller not only showed himself but also mediated and negotiated, winning for himself from time to time the name of "bapak" or "father" as recognition of the authority he held.

In the Belgian Congo colonial policy also inclined toward indirect administration. The institution of the native chieftaincy became the basic administrative unit, as defined by decrees issued in 1906 and 1910. Each such unit was submitted to the authority of a single chief who was selected according to existing local custom and who thereupon participated in an "investiture" ceremony

[10] Margery Perham, "A Re-Statement of Indirect Rule," *Africa*, VII, 2 (July 1934), pp. 325, 331, 334.
[11] A. D. A. de Kat Angelino, *Le Problème colonial.* Vol. II: *Les Indes Néerlandaises* (The Hague, 1932), p. 106.

whereby he received his powers from the Belgian authorities in return for which he promised his loyalty to them. The Director of Native Policy in the Belgian Colonial Ministry in 1932 summed up Belgian purposes as follows: "On the one hand this policy provides the advantage of allowing the progressive evolution of the natives within the framework of their own civilization; on the other hand, it allows us to administer our immense colonial empire with little effort and at the least cost." [12]

The French, torn in theory and practice between their procrustean policy of assimilation and their more recently devised policy of association, remained indecisive, but tended to opt officially for association in the postwar era. Before World War I, assimilation had already been attacked. As a political principle it had implied colonial centralization and unity, with all power emanating from Paris; as a cultural principle, it had stressed the paramountcy of French civilization and the need to illuminate the darkest recesses of the empire with the light of French rationalism. If practiced faithfully—but it never was—the theory would have led to the absorption of the French colonies into an empire one and indivisible, politically and culturally homogeneous.

Viewing the extent and variety of the new empire, many colonial analysts denounced assimilation as a vain and vague idea emphasizing universalism in a world of political and cultural particularities. They wished colonial policy to vary according to local needs and to be based on the principle of cooperation, not conversion. Al-

[12] Robert Reisdorff in *L'Essor économique belge: L'Expansion coloniale* (Brussels, 1932), p. 134.

ready proof of these new tendencies was given by colonial administrators far from the metropolitan scene and debate. In Madagascar, General Gallieni began what he called a *politique des races*, in which the use of local officials in the administration of the territory was advocated. "All administrative organization must follow the country in its natural development," Gallieni pronounced. In Morocco, General Lyautey, a protégé and admirer of Gallieni, successfully pursued a similar tack. He put it this way: "This agreeable and candid association of the two races is the best and surest guarantee of the future in Morocco. Nothing durable is based on force." Compared with the lamentable history of Algeria, where a desultory policy of assimilation was followed, the methods of Gallieni and Lyautey seemed crowned with success and worthy of imitation.

Now, in the postwar period, this French version of indirect rule became widely defined as a policy of association. It was explained as follows:

Politically, association finds its best form in the system of the protectorate which leaves the natives the major avenues of power, but which places at strategic intersections European administrators to whom the rights of initiative and veto pertain.

Economically, it establishes between native and European an indispensable collaboration; the latter is responsible for the conception, direction and scientific discovery of the colonial system; the former for carrying out the work.[13]

[13] Leon Baréty, "La Politique indigène de la France," in Brenier, Baréty *et al.*, *La Politique coloniale de la France* (Paris, 1924), pp. 76–77.

With this definition the supporters of Lugard's policy might agree, although they would have been chary of the still obvious directional role assigned the French colonial officer. And in its practice, they would have noticed the still prevailing French tendency toward direct administration at the top. Although association was practiced in West Africa and in Indochina, in Tunisia and Morocco the French moved toward more, rather than less, interference and direct control.

Direct or indirect rule, there was the question. If the former inclined toward cultural assimilation and disrespect of native institutions, the latter inclined toward opportunism and an attitude of do-nothingness. Before the attempt to mold colonial societies in the European image the "Lugardians" recoiled with horror. They desired no blatant violation of native customs and institutions; they believed in separate—and perhaps dissimilar—evolution. What they truly aspired to was a delicate balance between a general retention of local cultures and sufficient governmental modification by the colonial administrators to urge the native peoples forward. Margery Perham, as Lugard and others, realized how difficult this objective was, but she believed it could be achieved.

It seldom was, however. Too often indirect rule led to stagnation, to the freezing of traditional elites in power at a time when social mobility and the growth of potentially new elites were increasing. It thus tended to retard rather than accommodate social change. Furthermore, indirect rule may have been satisfactory where there was a rather elaborate pre-existing administrative structure which extended over a large territory of many people—

as did the Fulani one in Northern Nigeria—but in tribal Africa, authority was often widely diffused and limited; administrative units were small. Here indirect rule had little foundation upon which to operate. Finally, and most important, indirect rule, whatever its theoretical justification, tended to become an economical administrative device by which European authority could be brought easily down to the local level. Both French and Belgians established "native" chiefs in regions to which they were originally alien or even undesired; and this was done only for administrative convenience, not because of any sound anthropological reasoning. The colonial territory was first and foremost an administrative unit; social and political considerations were secondary and were primarily significant as they favorably affected the European task. Given these circumstances, the Europeans could not help but interfere with local customs and institutions and could not avoid making indirect rule only an administrative technique.

Perhaps the changing European colonial attitudes which partly forced the transformation of imperialism in these interwar years can here best be summed up by recapitulating the diachronic description of colonial history provided by the Dutch theorist A. D. A. de Kat Angelino.[14] Although sweeping in its scope, this brief description will hold up as well as any such generalization. It proposes a three-stage development of colonial attitudes. First, there is a period in which the European colonialists expressed either indifference or blatant racial superiority toward their native charges; then there is a second

[14] Angelino, *op. cit.*, Vol I: *Principes et méthodes*, pp. 256–259.

period in which the dominant objective was assimilation, a time when the colonizing power wished to endow its subject peoples with its institutions, customs, and way of life; finally, there occurred a period of synthesis in which assimilative tendencies were restrained, with the principal effort being directed toward the harmonization of colonial-native abilities and institutions while respect was maintained for indigenous cultural evolution. To de Kat Angelino, as to most of the significant colonial theorists of the 1920's and 1930's, imperialism was in this third, or international phase, that era when the common good of humanity was placed above any particular national interests, when the concept of the Sacred Trust of Civilization was to be properly capitalized.

Were it possible to write that these very theories, endowed with a certain nobility and high purpose, were effectively converted into workable colonial practice, the history of imperialism would be less dismal than it now appears. Without impugning the motives of the colonial theorists, we can say that their theories remained elevated, indeed removed from, colonial realities. The growing awareness of the need for colonial responsibility met with too little tangible support. The chief reason for this unfortunate outcome can perhaps best be described in terms of an inverted ratio: as a sense of colonial responsibility grew, colonial power declined; or, as colonial power declined, a sense of colonial responsibility grew. The particular order is difficult to determine. Whatever it was, the dominant political and economic position of prewar Europe was a thing of the past at the very time the European colonial theorists and administrators hoped to use this position most constructively.

Many colonial thinkers had come to the conclusion that considerable direct state aid was needed. "The great colonizer is the state," said one in 1910.[15] To fight disease and illiteracy, to develop raw materials and local industry, to administer to the needs of colonial peoples effectively, funds were needed, and these could not be demanded easily of private enterprise. This particular thought crystallized into coherent policy in the minds of some interwar colonial administrators, but everywhere it encountered formidable obstacles to its realization.

The colonial endeavor had been predicated since the late nineteenth century upon the principle of local financial autonomy: each colony was to pay its own way, to be little or no burden on state and taxpayer. The chief means of equipping colonies was, therefore, not the inclusion of such expenses in annual national budgets, but the floating of loans, generally in the form of colonial government bond issues, issues often underwritten by the home government to make them more attractive. This form of financing was not unsuccessful, as subscription to such bonds had a certain popularity in France and England, where both banks and private individuals responded. The great difficulty involved in such a method of capitalizing colonial infrastructures was the relatively modest and irregular sums that were amassable. The extensive and long-range goals prescribed by postwar colonial administrators would have required both massive and regular capital investment.

[15] Harmand, *op. cit.*, p. 150.

Only in the domain of railroad building had the colonial powers moved with financial zestfulness. Both governmental and private support was sufficient to endow most of the colonies with at least the rudiments of a modern transportation system. Rhodes had once commented that rails were less expensive than guns and went farther. Most colonial administrators agreed with him, seeing the railroad as a means by which to subdue the population and also to unify the colonial domain for economic and administrative purposes.

While the home governments did provide the colonial regions with direct financial support, this generally went for what has been called the "expenses of sovereignty": maintenance of armies and forts, administration, and public services such as the post and telegraph. At no time prior to the end of World War II was there a well-coordinated and well-financed plan for colonial development offered. Schemes such as Sarrault's *mise en valeur* were not realized, for none of the European governments were willing to endorse financially the statement made by Albert Girault, a French university professor, in 1895: "The colonial question has become a question of public works."

Now in the interwar period colonial development hit another obstacle. The spurt of economic activity which aroused the colonies in the 1920's was followed by the agonizing lull of the Depression '30s. Ill at ease in their search for solutions to the economic crisis at home—how advanced the economic activities of the New Deal seem by comparison—the European colonial powers often sought economic solace in their empires by means of the simple expedient of cutting budgets. Nor were all colonial administrators appalled by this turn of events. Governor-General Pasquier announced to the Grand Council of Indochina in 1931 that he was trimming the budget and justified his action in these words: "In Indochina it appears that we saw on too grand a scale and that we believed the country richer than it was. We rather lightly got involved in expenses and enterprises that were beyond the financial capacity of the country." The Belgian colonial writer Octave Louwers turned the Depression into something of inspiration when he remarked that budgetary stringency was not at all a bad thing:

We should not excessively regret this, for everywhere, here more, there less, the colonial nations have pursued the development of their new countries at a fast pace. The native populations have been singularly stirred! One would not dare say that this was always for their well-being, and it is perhaps not a bad thing that this great activity should be followed for some years by consolidation in order to allow things to settle. Crises often have salutary effects.[16]

And so plans were either not made or were shelved. The Belgians did nothing toward economic planning, and the Portuguese, under the new dictatorship of Salazar, principally prided themselves on balancing their colonial budgets. The British did introduce a Colonial Development Act in 1929 which led to the allocation of a

[16] Octave Louwers, *Le Problème financier et le problème économique au Congo belge* (Brussels, 1933), p. 25.

lonely one million pounds annually for that purpose. And the French, in imitation of the British move, proposed in 1934 a "National Fund for the Public Equipment of Overseas France," but the plan was hung up in Parliament for several years, finally expiring in 1937. In 1940 both countries seemed ready to move ahead again. French officials rehabilitated their idea of national funding, but wartime defeat ended any further serious consideration of it. The British did succeed in introducing a more generous and far-reaching Colonial Development and Welfare Act which set aside five million pounds annually for five years, but here, too, there were wartime hindrances.

From this assessment one should not conclude that money did not move into the colonies for the purpose of agrarian or industrial development. The chief financial support for such endeavors came from private enterprise, but this tended to be concentrated in a very few economic activities and areas, such as mining in South Africa, oil in Indonesia, rubber in Indochina. Here were centers of European-directed and -manned industry and agriculture. Such activities benefited first and foremost the Europeans, both those on the spot who worked them and those at home who owned them.

The resulting economic imbalance of this sort of activity is most vividly seen in colonial Africa. Between 1885 and 1936, for instance, of funds invested in Africa (and the total did not exceed six billion dollars), 42 per cent found their way into the Union of South Africa. Half a continent away, the enormous block of land constituting

French West Africa received but a paltry 3 per cent of these funds. British colonies like the Gold Coast and Nigeria were able to support themselves through their export trade, and, as is well known, the Belgian Congo remained financially buoyant thanks to the rich copper veins exploited by the Union Minière du Haut Katanga. Yet it was the vast majority of African territories and peoples under colonial control which remained underdeveloped.

True enough, money was not everything in the economic improvement of such lands. The process of modernization is a necessary combination of factors which include—beyond capital in its diverse forms—sound administration, internal markets and popular demands, effective governmental planning or a rich entrepreneurial class, and an educated populace. In the development of colonial economies the economic prejudices and needs of the colonial powers were paramount, those of the local region, incidental. From the European point of view complementary evolution was desired: the colonial region was incorporated into the national economy somewhat as an adjunct which provided raw materials for the metropolitan industrial complex and additional markets for its products. It seemed that the old notion of the *Pacte colonial* still lingered on in European thinking.

As a result of this lopsided arrangement, colonial economic development was primarily of an external not an internal sort: export economies with single corps ("monocultures") or with single extractive industries became the basis for whatever local prosperity was enjoyed. Industrial Europe had a powerful attraction on the agrarian and unsophisticated economies of the colonial world, and, as they were drawn outward, they were left underdeveloped inward.

All of the economic factors accounted for above require consideration, but let us now return to our earlier premise. Sound economic planning was not a post-World War II discovery. By the 1930's, as Sarraut's *La Mise en valeur des colonies françaises* indicates, colonial administrators realized the need for massive state aid to assure the success of the Dual Mandate idea, to modernize their possessions, and to equip them for the twentieth-century world. But a calcified fiscal policy, the dreadful distractions of the Depression and of the rise of totalitarianism, and the still optimistic belief that time was on their side, led the European colonial powers to do little toward the implementation of the plans that so many administrators longed to see undertaken.

If the history of imperialism abounds in irony, there is no more striking twist than this: the real effort toward the *mise en valeur* of the colonies occurred only after 1945, when the colonial epoch was drawing to a close. Then considerable investment flowed from colonial power to colonial territory, with the British further implementing their Development Act, with the Belgian government inaugurating a ten-year plan for the Congo in 1950, and with the French establishing an elaborate fiscal scheme known by its initials as FIDES (Fonds d'investissement pour le développement économique et social). Even Portugal, tardy because dormant and smug, made a feeble effort in this direction with its National Development Plan of 1953 in which Angola and Mozambique were included.

Perhaps, however, the colonial theorists were asking too much of the pre-World War II governments. In effect what they were suggesting was not only colonial development but colonial welfare, the need for the state to participate fully in the economic and social development of the empire. This very thought rebounded against the still-standing wall of laissez-faire economics and Lockean politics, and came into opposition with the rather time-worn idea of colonial pay-as-you-go. This was still a world in which the only serious state planning was done by the Communists and the Nazis, and their examples were not about to be emulated. Only with the belated success of Keynesian economics, with the advent of the Welfare State in Europe, and with the threat of a powerful Russian imperialism—a threat which, among other things, caused Marshall Plan funds to flood into Europe and then to flow out again to the colonies—were the colonial powers to loosen their purse strings and do what they had long said they would do.

The outline of the last phase of overt imperialism was already sketched before World War II so vividly highlighted it. As colonial theory changed and as colonial policy wavered and hesitated, nationalism in this Third World gained strength and direction. Within a few years the initiative would pass from the European administrators to the native elites as the events of a troubled world seemed to militate against the continuation of overseas empire.

5 . THE END OF EMPIRE

Within little more than a decade after the end of World War II, European colonial empires had all but totally vanished. In an unanticipated symmetry the end was like the beginning. Portugal, this time by default, once again emerged as Europe's greatest colonial power. With Mozambique and Angola still firmly placed under her rule, she now governed more alien land than France and England, who had but the spare remnants of their glorious empires of yesteryear.

This devolution of colonial empire has been a historical process which few others in this century can match in importance or in dispatch. Broadly speaking, the arrival of dozens of new nations, yesterday politically subservient colonies, on the world scene has enlarged and complicated international politics and has brought new political consciousness and hope to millions of persons whose range of interest was heretofore limited to communal affairs. Furthermore, the relative ease with which this change was effected is arresting. Whatever the extent of opinions about the obstinate desire of Europeans to retain their empire, these same Europeans allowed the transfer of power to be accomplished quickly, although the process was not without its many aggravated moments and accompanying bloodshed.

There were a number of wars of colonial devolution. Indonesia, Indochina, and Algeria were the unfortunate battlegrounds on which an aroused local population fought ardently and violently against colonial troops whose mission was to crush the insurgents and to restore something of the colonial power's former political control. Elsewhere in the dying colonial world there were outbursts, as in Malaya, Kenya, and the Belgian Congo. But if these wars and struggles are considered on the grand colonial scale, with all the emerging nations around the globe included, their number is significant because of its rather modest magnitude. Southeast Asia was the region of the most intense belligerency on the part of the Europeans, but almost all of Africa, the former mandated and trust territories, and many of the scattered islands in the Caribbean and the Pacific received their independence without major military altercations. It is true that frequently the granting of independence barely preceded serious local political disturbances—which were, in turn, frequently the reason for the precipitous European action—but the point remains that clashes between colonizer and colonized were far less frequent in the process of colonial devolution than in the comparable process leading to national independence and republicanism in Europe.

However belatedly and however reluctantly, the European colonial powers realized the evolution of their possessions to statehood.

When Europe went to war in 1939 its colonial empires still stood firm and appeared to be a source of great strength. When Europe slowly emerged from the wasteland of that war nearly six years later, empire was no longer certain. The war had changed the disposition of world power; and the war had aroused colonial peoples to a new consciousness of their subordinate status.

Quite obviously, no European colonial power, except England, had come out of the war victoriously, and even England had paid a most heavy price for her heroic resistance to fascism. Holland, Belgium, and France fell quickly under Nazi domination; Italy was soon controlled by Germany and not long after overrun by American armies. Everywhere the myth of European colonial superiority and the belief in the solidity of European colonial rule were shattered.

In the Far East, where colonial nationalism had already led an exuberant life before the war, the Japanese effectively and ruthlessly swept away European power. The citadel of Singapore, something of an imperialist kingpin, was taken with great ease; Malaya and Burma were invaded and conquered; and Indochina succumbed, with the French first conceding to the Japanese and then being completely displaced by them in early 1945. The Japanese, in their hopes of creating an old-fashioned empire behind the façade of their Co-Prosperity Sphere, enlisted the support of the local populations who, like the Burmese, momentarily looked upon them as kindred brothers and as liberators. In Indonesia, Sukarno was made a collaborator, and in Indochina, Bao Dai was compelled by the Japanese to declare his country's independence from France. As the war progressed, however, and as Japanese control became more stringent, resistance movements arose and rallied nationalists in most of the overrun countries, nationalists who now wished to eject the Japanese and furthermore guarantee that the Europeans would not return. Sizable military forces were built up in this way and were to complicate, if not prevent, the reinstallation of colonial institutions. General Giap of the Vietminh, for instance, had an army of some 10,000 men under his command when the war ended, and this army, enlarged, was to defeat France at Dien Bien Phu in 1954.

The Europeans, coming back to their old Asian possessions in 1945, were rudely awakened to a realization of the new political facts, but still were unwilling to accept their significance. Paul Mus in his *Destin de l'Union française* comments that the returning French were dismayed to see the statue of Paul Bert, one of France's great colonial figures, overturned in a square of Hanoi. The Dutch, reappearing in Indonesia to replace the

British, who had occupied that land after the retreating Japanese, observed the red and white flag of the newly declared Republic of Indonesia flying over public buildings, but they chose to ignore it and to fight, as did the French, to retain their Asiatic empire. The forces of Asian nationalism, recharged by the Japanese occupation and then the resistance to it, were, however, much too strong to be pushed aside or even seriously compromised by the European colonial powers.

If the war made the colonial situation impossible in the Far East, it made it precarious in North Africa. Invading German armies, supporting a weak Italian effort, rolled across much of North Africa as if it were a castle of sand and seriously threatened the existence of the British in Egypt. Subsequently invading Americans in Morocco and Algeria brought an anticolonial spirit along with their superior arms and helped arouse a strong sentiment against imperialist rule among the local populations. In Morocco the nationalist Istiqlal Party appeared in 1944, announced Morocco's adherence to the principles of the Atlantic Charter, and demanded Moroccan independence of France. In Algeria similar sentiments had already been expressed. By 1943 Ferhat Abbas had changed his political tack and was heading a pro-Algerian movement. His *Algerian Manifesto* of 1943 announced: "Henceforth, a Moslem Algerian asks to be nothing other than a Moslem Algerian." With the forceful removal of Italy from the realm of colonial powers, Libya presented a political problem, one which the United Nations solved quite simply by granting that

117

desert land independence in 1951, thus causing both inspiration and irritation among the still colonial-dependent territories of the Maghreb.

One further factor which both complicated the colonial situation and frustrated the colonial powers was the wartime ascendancy of the United States and the Soviet Union. While both of these states soon developed a Manichaean approach to international affairs in the postwar era, with Russia seeing the United States as the source of all secular evil and the United States returning the compliment, they did share in common an anticolonial and anti-imperialist sentiment.

The United States enjoyed a long-established anticolonial tradition. Not only did she have the well-used historical example of her own revolt against the British colonial system, but also she had evolved a diplomatic style which depended on democratic idealism, as Wilson's attitude at the time of Versailles illustrates. Furthermore, a sense of empathy for the underdog could be easily aroused among the American public, as, for example, the enthusiasm over the visit of Louis Kossuth after the failure of the Hungarian Revolution of 1848 illustrates. Although the United States had her fever of overseas imperialism at the end of the nineteenth century, this soon subsided; in its stead again grew a suspicion of old-fashioned power politics and the European colonialism characteristic of them. As World War II concluded, the American government gave expression to this anticolonial sentiment. During the Cairo and Teheran Conferences held during the winter of 1943–1944, President Roosevelt proposed that Indochina be placed under international control to assure that the French colonial regime would not be reinstituted there. Then the government promptly upheld its promise to grant the Philippines independence in 1946.

While the United States was soon in the embarrassing position of providing ardent support to France and Great Britain while trying at the same time to maintain a positive attitude toward decolonization, she did not initially seem to equivocate and, in fact, inspired genuine enthusiasm among the colonial peoples. Several examples of this could readily be mentioned, but perhaps the most interesting is that provided by the Vietnamese republic created by Ho Chi Minh in 1945. It was to an anticolonial United States that Ho turned, assured in his own mind that the United States and China would be the main sources of foreign support in his struggle against the French. On the very day of Vietnamese independence General Giap, who was to direct the North Vietnamese military effort against South Vietnam and the United States, called the relations between China, the United States, and Viet Nam "intimate," and said that he found this subject "a pleasant duty to dwell upon." [1]

There is probably little need to stress the Soviet Union's official attitude toward imperialism in general and colonialism in particular. Certainly one can denounce the attitude of the Soviets as hypocritical: European overseas imperialism was violently berated while Russia herself absorbed significant portions of Eastern and Central Europe without much embarrassment. But this action in

[1] Cited in Ellen Hammer, *The Struggle for Indochina* (Stanford, 1958), p. 131.

no way deterred the official ideology which derived directly from Lenin's work on imperialism. Stalin, who wished to inherit the mantle of intellectual-political leader, embellished the Leninist doctrine. In 1925, speaking to the students of the University of the Peoples of the East, he outlined the process by which anticolonialism and Communism would march hand in hand. With the establishment of the Party, and the enlistment of intellectuals, peasants, and workers, war would be waged both against the colonialists and the bourgeoisie so that the colonial order would be overthrown and a proletarian government established in its stead. However, Soviet thought in later years tended to move along the lines already established by the Second Congress of the Communist International (1920) which enunciated what has since been called the principle of the two-stage revolution: initial cooperation between the "nationalist bourgeoisie" and the Communists in the struggle for national liberation, to be followed by the revolutionary triumph of the Communists once imperialist control has been destroyed.

The Russian doctrine was not without its appeal. It offered both an explanation of the causes of imperialism and a means to the destruction of imperialism. Although most of the regions undergoing decolonization followed no set ideology with rigor, some of the leaders borrowed freely from Communist thought and adapted it to their own uses. For instance, Kwame Nkrumah, who was given to creating parables and coining slogans, exclaimed: "Peoples of the colonies, unite—the working men of all countries are behind you." This statement, of course, has a familiar ring, and the argument preceding it was quite faithful to the Leninist tradition.[2]

Elsewhere, Communism provided a rallying cry for guerrillas who engaged both colonial powers and legitimate independent governments in battle. They fought against the United States and the Philippine government, against the British in Malaya, and, of course, against the French in Indochina. In these areas Communism and the nationalist movement momentarily blended together and thus increased the trouble caused the colonial powers. While it would be erroneous to assume that the Kremlin was slyly giving support to all of these Communist movements—most of them were of local origin and were originally ignored by Russia, which was concentrating on Eastern Europe and the Cold War in the late 1940's—Communist ideology, like the American anticolonial tradition, was a source of moral strength and popular argument. It provided a vision of the future against which the oppressive present could be compared.

It would be easy to magnify the importance of the anticolonialist ideology of the superstates in the process of decolonization. Moreover, it must be recalled that the Cold War made Soviet-American cooperation a near impossibility and, indeed, occupied their attention with other than colonial problems as such. Yet they did join in fact if not in spirit on occasion on this issue. The most unusual example of their efforts was the joint condemnation of the Anglo-French invasion of Egypt in 1956, an invasion that would have warmed the hearts of all nine-

[2] Kwame Nkrumah, *Towards Colonial Freedom* (London, 1962). See particularly, pp. 42–43.

teenth-century Jingoists but which quickly incurred the wrath and irritation of most of the contemporary states. This ill-timed adventure was brought to a speedy halt, no doubt chiefly because of American remonstrances, but with Soviet support nonetheless.

The anticolonial sentiment which both powers expressed was hardly limited to themselves, however. Indeed, it was far more vociferously stated by other nations. Latin America, India, Egypt, Ethiopia, and the Eastern European states joined in a chorus of official denunciation. They found their best forum to be the United Nations.

Born of World War II itself, the United Nations further internationalized the colonial problem, as it took up where the League of Nations stopped and as it proceeded to broaden and strengthen the League tradition in colonial matters. Chapters XI, XII, and XIII of the UN Charter continued where Articles 22 and 23 of the League had left off. But it was Article 73 of Chapter XI which contained the general principles and instructions by which nonautonomous territories were to be governed. Again the notion of sacred trust was refurbished, and again the responsibility of the administering power to assist the dependent territory to arrive at self-administration was enunciated. Paragraph "e" was the real innovation—and the later source of contention. It stated that the powers responsible for administration of nonautonomous territories were to communicate regularly to the Secretary General, as information, statistical and other technical data relative to the economic and social conditions in these territories. Paragraph "e" thus introduced, but did not clearly define, a principle of direct colonial accounting, and this principle was pushed with vigor by the anticolonial forces in the UN and equally resisted by the colonial forces. The problem was particularly complicated by the lack of a limiting definition of nonautonomous territory. Article 73 vaguely described the dominating states and the nonautonomous territories as: "the Members of the United Nations who have or who assume responsibility to administer territories whose populations do not yet completely administer themselves." The major colonial powers did include most of their colonial possessions within this category and were willing to give the information requested, but balked when members of the UN tried to include political information (numbers of indigenous population participating in local government, for instance) and also tried to establish the right of UN committees to visit their nonautonomous territories.

The anticolonial forces of the United Nations were trying to obtain greater international control over the disposition of colonies, while the colonial powers countered by frequently attempting to reinstate their old principle that colonial relations were simply dual: those between colonial power and colonial possession. This particular division of sentiment was to be complicated and extended by the Cold War, thus making the UN role often a confusing and a minor one. Yet the UN had its triumphs. Under its aegis the Indonesian war was brought to a successful conclusion in 1949 when the Dutch recognized Indonesian independence. Its observers watched over the elections in the Cameroons and Togoland. It established the deadline for independence for Somaliland and saw that deadline realized. And through its energetic and determined Secretary-General, Dag Hammarskjöld, it played an active part in bringing Moise Tshombe's Katanga province back into the new Congo nation in 1960.

There were many incidents of failure, too. France managed to keep Indochina and Algeria out of UN affairs for some time, insisting in the first instance that Indochina was granted independence in 1948 and hence no longer was accountable under 73e, and invoking in the second instance the principle that Algeria was an integral part of France and hence not within the purview of the UN. Until recently, Salazar's successful attempts —attempts, granted, only successful because of British-American acquiescence—to keep Angola off the UN agenda have also been a source of irritation to most nations of the world. Finally, the question of South Africa's mandate of Southwest Africa (the former German colony), aggravated by the institution of *apartheid*, remained an unresolved legal question until 1966. However, the only solution reached so far is a paper one revoking the mandate. South Africa's intention to retain Southwest Africa, by force if necessary, clearly indicates that this problem is still acute.

All in all, the United Nations principally figured in the process of decolonization somewhat as a Greek chorus, commenting on the action which was taking place on the central stage, now admonishing, now foretelling. In so doing, the UN attracted world attention to colonial problems and tended to pique the conscience of

European governments already ridden by self-doubt and, also, it is true, by concern for the welfare of their still dependent peoples.

The UN illustrated changing world attitudes and changing world power, both of which suggested that some sort of new colonial deal was in order. Yet what is perhaps most interesting in retrospect was the minimal amount of innovation introduced by the Europeans into postwar colonial policy. Most of the powers conceded the need for reforms and indeed introduced them, primarily in the economic realm. But everywhere there was a persistence to follow along familiar paths. The real period of innovation in colonial policy had been the interwar years. Theories and ideas then adumbrated were now given sharper form and were implemented in practice. What this earlier development therefore suggests is this: even if World War II had not occurred, colonial reform in the direction of more autonomy and greater participation by local populations in the administration of empire would have been introduced. To be sure, there would have been no sense of urgency or of compulsion to make such changes occur rapidly or extensively. War, that dreadful social reformer, was responsible for the quickened pace, as it was also partially responsible for the final outcome of political independence.

Of all the colonial powers, Great Britain was best able to accommodate to the changing times, this principally because her colonial theory and, of late, her colonial practice were most compatible with new colonial demands. Autonomy and independence within the loose framework of the Commonwealth was an accepted British objective.

Although Winston Churchill had categorically stated that he had not become prime minister in order to preside over the dissolution of the British Empire, his Labourite successors were more pliable and more realistic. Following upon Indian independence they made serious attempts to provide a timetable of self-government and possibly independence for all portions of their empire. Burma, Ceylon, and Malaya all followed India, as the West Indies were to do soon also. In Africa, the Gold Coast set its own fast pace toward political freedom, one which found British constitutional reforms antiquated at the very moment of their inauguration. Yet the comparatively smooth, quick, and intelligent devolution of British empire should not lead one to the conclusion that the British necessarily wanted it this way.

The Labour government, despite its philosophic and political origins, was not intent upon swiftly winding up the colonial enterprise once and for all. Labour's attitude toward the colonies was essentially a humanitarian one, and now in power, the Labour government attempted to reform, to regenerate, to prepare, but not simply to release British dependencies. As Arthur Creech Jones, Labour Secretary of State for Colonies, said in the *New Fabian Essays* of 1959:

In the situation of 1945 the colonial peoples would have protested against the withdrawal by Britain unless they felt secure and strong enough to carry the burden of their own Government. As it proved, within a few years the educated men in the colonies began to demand freedom from alien control; but in 1945 conditions were not ripe for British renunciation.

The notion of obligation still persisted, but with good intention and often good results Labour did its best to assure a smooth transition from empire to statehood. When the Conservatives returned to power in 1950 they continued this policy, recognizing, as their leader Harold Macmillan was to declare, that the winds of change were blowing hard, even across Subsaharan Africa. Of course, Britain had a distinct advantage in the colonial tradition of dominion self-government. The Balfour statement of 1926, which became the essence of the Westminster Act of 1931, recognized the dominions as autonomous and equal units in the British Empire, or the British Commonwealth of Nations. Admission of South Africa and India to this select circle proved that the older notion of English-peopled, white-settlement colonies alone being granted dominion status had now expired. Therefore, as the dependencies were released from their colonial status, they were invited to embrace the Commonwealth cause, and most of them did do this. Retrospectively, almost all commentators on the history of British empire see the process of colonial devolution as inherent in the system which received its first clear inspiration from Burke and his East India Company speech on the concept of trust. According to Sir Ernest Barker, the trust concept as applied to empire had three concentric rings: the trust idea itself, the mandate, and indirect rule.[3] The fourth circle, one that did not seem so obvious

[3] Barker, *op. cit.*, pp. 64–71.

in 1941 when Barker expressed this idea, is, of course, independence within the Commonwealth.

The French were less able, or willing, to adjust to postwar conditions. In contrast to the British pattern, French colonial solutions appeared as patchwork. The historical persistence of old ideas and of old dreams, particularly that of "100,000,000 Frenchmen" residing in an empire one and indivisible, was strong and was never wholeheartedly discouraged. Yet many colonial administrators believed that a return to assimilationist practices would not be sound, and some even began to speak of imperial federation somewhat in imitation of their Channel neighbors.

The history of postwar French colonial policy begins with the Brazzaville Conference held in January and February of 1944. On this occasion the colonial administrators of the Subsaharan territories and French observers from Tunisia, Morocco, and Algeria were all assembled under the aegis of de Gaulle's provisional government sitting in Algiers. In a way the Conference set the tone for postwar French colonial policy, the two dominant notes being administrative decentralization and assimilation in matters of the rights and status of the individual. As René Pleven, the presiding officer of the Conference suggested, the war experience had taught French administrators the advantages to be derived from considerable local autonomy. The newly expressed desire was for a federative administrative system allowing for political decentralization, for local planning, but not for political independence. Moreover, colonial representation in France was to be increased, but by the means of a colonial or federal parliament. As a step in this direction, the Brazzaville Conference stated that the colonial territories would all be represented in the Constituent Assembly charged with the task of providing postwar France with a constitution. Yet in no manner did the Conference suggest any dissolution of empire. Its most famous words were the following:

The objectives of the civilizing effort accomplished by France in the colonies lead to the rejection of any idea of autonomy, of any possible evolution outside of the French bloc of empire; the eventual constitution of self-government in the colonies, no matter how far off, is rejected.

The two French constitutional conventions completing their work in 1946 produced documents which reveal the confusion of assimilationist and federative ideas of empire. Both documents contain contradictions and ambiguities which have interested and baffled legists. What remains significant about both, however, was the creation of a French Union which was at least nominally federative and which allowed for a variety of relationships between France and her dependencies. Under the accepted constitution of October 27, 1946, the French Union consisted of the French Republic (this including the metropolitan territory and the newly created "overseas departments" of Guadeloupe, Martinique, Guiana, and Réunion, and also the "overseas territories," chiefly the colonies of West and Equatorial Africa), the Associated States (the protectorate of Indochina and supposedly those of Tunisia and Morocco, although the latter two never joined), and the Associated Territories (the mandates of Togoland and Cameroon).[4] All but the Associated States were to have representation in the French National Assembly; the Associated States along with France were to sit on a High Council of the French Union, while all overseas and metropolitan territories were to be represented in an Assembly of the French Union. All, too, were to enjoy an ill-defined citizenship in the French Union, while all members of the French Republic —overseas departments and territories included—were to be French citizens.

Without sinking into the morass of opinion and interpretation surrounding the meaning of the new institutions, one can suggest that, while the Constitution of October 27, 1946, was sloppily worded and legally ambiguous, the tendencies of postwar colonial policy in it were clear.

First, a federation or a commonwealth was declared to be the general framework in which the various parts of the French colonial empire would be joined. As the Preamble of the Constitution states, "France forms with the overseas peoples a union founded on the equality of rights and of responsibilities, without distinction of race or religion." Second, the assimilationist tendency toward equality for all under the protecting umbrella of French institutions was also evident. The concepts of citizenship suggest this, for whatever else they may have meant,

[4] The complexity of the Algerian situation resulting principally from the demographic distribution of one million Europeans among an Arab and Berber population of eight million was such that Algeria was not included in the new arrangement of the French Union but was regulated by a special statute of September 20, 1947.

they did guarantee the individual rights prescribed in the constitution for all colonial peoples. Third, the dominant directing position of France in her colonial world was not to be abandoned. The Preamble to the Constitution also states: "Faithful to her traditional mission, France intends to lead the peoples whose freedom is entrusted to her to their self-administration and to the democratic conduct of their own affairs." Here, scarcely covered, is the old notion of *mission civilisatrice*.

In sum the Constitution tried to complement assimilation with federation, to allow for greater territorial autonomy while still insisting that the Union turn on metropolitan France. The results of this arrangement were ineffective and contradictory, with the outcome that the French Union as a truly federal body existed in name only, its two institutions, the High Council and the Assembly, moribund from the start.

Even General de Gaulle's solution to the colonial problem, to wit the French Community, while more liberal and flexible than its predecessor, originally allowed for no accommodation of those areas which chose independence over membership in the community. While the overseas territories were given the option and the means to withdraw from the community, independence was never considered a desideratum in de Gaulle's eyes.

Among the lesser colonial powers a similar continuity with prewar policy is obvious. Belgium rather laconically considered that political privileges and responsibilities should be commensurate with an individual's standard of living. On the merit of this logic, she assumed that economic development should continue to have priority. The industrialization of the Congo briskly proceeded through the efforts of the great concessionary companies like the Union Minière du Haut-Katanga, and individual incomes were raised. But the Congo was kept politically subservient in an authoritarian system which one author has described as Platonic, as, he argued, "is implicit in the sharp division, social and legal, between Belgian philosopher-kings and the mass of African producers." [5] Politics, in brief, were made to wait, with the unfortunate results that were to occur in the Congo beginning in 1960. Portugal, still counting time in centuries, pridefully remarked that her old African possessions were being integrated into the metropolitan body politic and thereupon made them legally overseas departments, all the while maintaining severe legal sanctions which assured the great mass of the local populations of being little more than disinherited peons. Not until rebellion broke out in Angola in 1961 were the Portuguese aroused from their idle reveries.

This lack of striking innovation in colonial policy immediately following upon the war years should not be construed—as it often has been by anticolonialists—to mean that the European powers were insensitive to the rising demands in Asia and Africa for self-determination and national independence. Rather it suggests a lack of fine appreciation of the vitality and purpose of the nationalist movements. The colonial powers were no longer dealing with small groups of rebels or frustrated

[5] Thomas Hodgkin, op. cit., p. 52.

politicians, but with political organizations highly directed from above and more and more popularly supported from below. In the classic sense revolutionary conditions were taking shape.

The European response in the last decade of overseas imperialism, which was the 1950's, was that of hasty efforts to prepare the chafing colonial peoples for independence. But even then the modes of thought and the plans of action employed were European-centered.

The general tendency of governments and colonial administrators was to consider political maturity, and hence independence, in terms of the European historical experience. The necessary preconditions were deemed to be: a functioning multiparty system, an able and dedicated bureaucracy, a literate electorate, and some degree of national economic viability. Of course these very characteristics were conspicuous in the colonial world by their absence prior to 1940, and critics have rightly blamed the colonial powers for failure to assure them earlier. But such an accusation does not really detract from the hardy, if belated, efforts to bring about their existence after the war.

The pace which the European maintained was not everywhere the same. In general, the Asian possessions arrived at independence well before a program could be elaborated and successfully implemented. The war in Indochina, the guerrilla activities in Malaya, the insistent demands of Burma for independence, and, of course, the most recent and imposing precedent of Philippine and Indian independence, were all complicating factors which allowed the colonial administrators and the home governments little choice but to transfer power as best they could.

In Africa the Europeans could still hope they had time on their side, as they could hope to profit belatedly from their recent and unpleasant Asian experiences. The obvious direction in which independence-preparation moved was toward constitutional reform. Greater participation by local populations in the governmental process was the first objective. Great Britain altered her administrative machinery so that local legislative assemblies became African in composition and responsible in authority. For instance, following upon the report of the Coussey Commission, established in 1949 for the purpose of providing the Gold Coast with constitutional reform, a legislature with almost all members chosen by the electoral process was installed and granted the right of executive dismissal, thus assuring both representative and responsible government. In 1952 Kwame Nkrumah became the first prime minister and was allowed to form the first African cabinet. Between 1952 and 1956 pressure from the Convention Peoples' Party, which Nkrumah headed and handily manipulated, induced more constitutional reforms so that in 1957 the Gold Coast Colony became the "sovereign, unitary republic" of Ghana.

The French, too, introduced legislative reforms, the most striking and controversial of which was the *Loi Cadre* (Enabling Act) of 1956, primarily drawn up by Gaston Deferre, Minister of Overseas France, and by Felix Houphouet-Boigny, minister without portfolio in the Guy Mollet government, and future president of the

Ivory Coast. The most significant feature of the decree was to give the popular-elected territorial assemblies in French Africa political power by allowing them to choose the cabinets which would have executive authority in each territory. Each territory also gained control of the local purse strings by being allowed to collect taxes and to utilize the revenues from them. Following in the persistent French tradition, the law left external affairs in the hands of the French, suggested no local political independence, but did assure greater African participation in the local decision-making processes.

These two particular examples, no doubt the most outstanding of the British and French efforts, do indicate that the colonial powers were introducing political changes and were responding to local pressures. Yet, even when inspired by good intentions,[6] the Europeans could not readily appreciate that colonial independence might be demanded and achieved in conditions far from those considered optimal. The national independence movements in Asia and Africa, but particularly in the latter region, were seen as premature because the European-prescribed political desiderata were far from being filled. Without these, ran the European argument, independence could well be meaningless, for it would lead to confusion, not freedom.

The colonial peoples observed and judged from a

[6] There has been criticism of the French *Loi Cadre* of 1956. Some analysts insist that in granting greater authority to the territorial assemblies and reducing that of the Grand Council of French West Africa, the French were purposely segmenting their West African colonies into small and ineffective political units, ultimately to be still dependent on France even after independence.

different perspective and could not appreciate this old and persistent European attitude.

For this much the whole world knows, that the right of a people to rule themselves does not depend on the generosity of the overlords, nor does it depend on the preparedness of the people. The truth, and this truth has never been seriously repudiated, is that any man has a right to break crockery in his own house. If he bungles he will soon learn how to set up things right. But the issue never arises whether any other man has the right to take occupation of the house on the grounds that the owner is unable to take good care of it. That would be a ludicrous suggestion.[7]

In these words a South African Negro journalist sharply answered the doubting Europeans and also dispelled the perplexing dilemma that the Earl of Cromer had conjured up some fifty years ago. The issue was no longer necessarily of good government, but strictly of self-government, of "Self-government now," as Nkrumah's successful political slogan read. Gladstone's liberal notion that the only way to know freedom is to have freedom gained new relevance in the seething colonial world, where it was difficult to refute and impossible to combat.

Social and economic betterment, autonomous government, greater imperial flexibility were hardly enough; political freedom almost everywhere seemed to be the only acceptable solution to the colonial problem in the eyes of the colonial elites. As has been pointed out on numerous occasions, the one aspect of modern communal existence which the Europeans continually denied their

[7] Lewis Nkosi, "The New Africans," *Nieman Reports*, XV, 4 (October 1961), 4.

colonial peoples until most recently was the privilege and responsibility of political decision-making. Politics, therefore, took on immense proportions. Everywhere the colonial elites insisted upon political control. "Seek ye first the political kingdom," announced Kwame Nkrumah, "and all else shall be added unto it."

Politics meant nationalism. In the second decade of the postwar era, when nationalism was looked upon as an anachronism in Europe, it was an up-to-date phenomenon in the colonial regions. Essentially a European importation compounded of liberal and revolutionary thought, colonial nationalism both took form and gave combat in opposition to European imperialist rule, much as European nationalism had done a century before in its struggle against the dynastic state.

Colonial nationalism was first and foremost a cohesive force through its negativeness, its anti-imperialism. Nationalists saw the European imperialists as the chief impediment to their political independence and economic modernization. The policy of imperialism, they concluded, had only been to subject and to hinder. For the nationalists the struggle was now one for political liberation. Such an ideology, if one may use the term, had the advantage of directing attention and activity against one easily discerned enemy and one simple cause of misfortune. Moreover, it had the advantage of arousing a sense of identity among the peoples who had hitherto been grouped together administratively but who seldom felt any commonality; a community of the oppressed was being born.

No contemporary author has offered a more forceful and arresting thesis—albeit it an exaggerated one—than Frantz Fanon in his bitter *Les Damnés de la terre*.[8] Basing his argument on the model provided in Georges Sorel's famous *Reflections on Violence*, Fanon contends that the history of colonialism began, continued, and ended as a series of acts of violence. The colonialist was the oppressor; he "never ceases to be the enemy, the antagonist, most precisely, the man to battle." In such a situation the colonized realized that the only way to attain freedom was by the violent, terrorist act. But these acts had their positive, their formative side also. "The mobilization of the masses, when it occurs during the war of liberation, introduces in each mind the notion of a common cause, of national destiny, of collective history."

There is a serious danger of generalizing too widely about the number of elements solidifying nationalism and about the extent of national unity in the new states. In truth, many of them most recently emerging from colonial status are but ministates or micronations, splinters of large land and ethnic masses, having no rhyme or reason other than that deriving from colonial division. They happen to be simply because the colonial configurations were so drawn. Botswana (Bechuanaland), Lesotho (Basutoland), and The Gambia in Africa, all now enjoying nominal sovereignty, are the most grotesque examples of the vagaries of colonial independence. They cannot hope to be nations, to forge a common future, to acquire the necessary attributes of statehood any more

[8] Frantz Fanon, *Les Damnés de la terre* (Paris, 1961). See Chapter 1, "De la violence."

than can Monaco or Liechtenstein in Europe. At best their nationhood consists of a cabinet, a flag, and a seat in the United Nations. Nor is this last statement meant to be derisive but rather to point up one pathetic aspect of the process of decolonization.

The Europeans have been accused of Balkanization, of dividing Africa and other regions perhaps into small political segments incapable of independent existence and therefore easily susceptible to foreign influence, if not control. For instance, if French West Africa had acquired national existence as a single unit—or even as two units, as Leopold Sedar Senghor of Senegal had desired—its economic viability, its demographic size, and its very land mass would have assured it greater political significance. Divided as it now is into some eight states, none with a population of more than a few million, and with economic resources widely separated and certain countries landlocked, this area of West Africa is politically and economically weak.

It will do no good, from the perspective of the people formerly under colonialism, to suggest that the Europeans often created larger units than pre-existed, that they reduced the number of political entities from hundreds to dozens. And it will do no good to suggest that in their present state of economic development and with their relatively light industry, these states would enjoy few larger markets and would increase their industrial output but little if they extended much more in size. What one must everywhere reckon with are the telling arguments: (1) that, if the European imperialists had wished, they could have amalgamated many of their colonies into more rational state units prior to their departure; (2) that, if the European imperialists had wished, they could have developed diversified economies, instead of the generally existing single-crop or single-industry economy.

Serious arguments have therefore been raised about the disadvantages caused by the European granting of nationhood, or its encouragement, in administrative colonial units either too small or already segmented so that they could not become meaningful states and nations. Many of the "pan" movements, such as Pan-Arabism and Pan-Africanism, are based on the premise that the future greatness and significance of the former colonial regions lies in their transcending nationalism to something of federalism. While nationhood may be the initial means by which to mobilize political, social, and economic forces latent in the region, the real social and cultural future lies with something more fundamental and profound, something more historical, reaching beyond and below the colonial experience and its immediate nationalist legacy. This may be *négritude*, for instance, (the "negroness" of the African), or the Islamic religion and culture.

Colonial nationalism, while part of a universal historical movement which has characterized political developments of the last two and a half centuries, has had its unique aspects. In at least one respect it is the reverse of the nineteenth-century European version: in the former instance, future political boundaries were already determined by the configurations of each colony. Thus the framework of the nation existed before the spirit of nationalism was infused into it. In the latter instance, the spirit of nationalism most often preceded any political demarcation of the nation—as in Germany or Italy. The colonial elites were, therefore, confronted with the task of creating a nationalism after the fact. In general they did so by delving far into the past, by going beyond both the immediate colonial past and the pre-colonial past just before that. Sukarno of Indonesia returned to the fourteenth-century Madjapahit Empire, celebrated more in poetry than in fact, which supposedly embraced much of the Southeast Asian world from the Philippines to the Malayan Peninsula. President Nkrumah selected the name Ghana in reference to the great Empire of Ghana which sprawled across much of West Africa between the ninth and twelfth centuries. President Senghor hit upon the name of Mali for the soon aborted federation between the Senegal and the Soudan, partly to please Modibo Keita of Soudan, who traced his ancestry back to a great Malian ruler, and partly to strike a meaningful historical note, for Mali, like Ghana before it, was a West African empire of great import.

In each historical selection cited above the name and the state evoked derived from glorious epochs when the ancestors of the present generation of newly liberated peoples ruled majestically, commanded respect, and were subservient to no one. This search for a historical past as the means to a meaningful national future is an old and respected nationalist enterprise. Michelet rummaged through the Middle Ages to hunt for France; Treitschke militantly marshaled the dead Hohenzollerns to account for Germany. The number of tales still current in the United States about George Washington or Abraham Lincoln suggests that America, too, has its share of mythical unity. Now Asian and African nations are looking backward for the roots of contemporary identity. Of course, much fiction has been mixed with fact, but the prescribed objective, a community of common interest with which to forge national unity, is a legitimate one.

While the power of nationalism became positive as it galvanized disparate ethnic and cultural groups into a common struggle against imperialism and in a search for a common past, its chief effect was still to deny the legitimacy of colonial rule. At first glance, this legitimacy may seem to have been starkly that of the sword. But no colonial regime had ever reduced its authority to such a narrow base. The professed justification for colonial rule had all along been its necessity: the European was needed to maintain a local *pax*, to prevent internecine warfare, to exterminate disease, to develop agriculture and trade, to educate. European colonial legitimacy was like that of *ancien régime* Europe, based not on popular support or popular sovereignty, but on imposed order, on the effective regulation of social and economic life by administrative and police means. Colonial rule rested fundamentally on what political scientists have labeled the legitimacy of command, rather than the legitimacy of consent.

Granted imperialist authority was that of command, it would have been unsuccessful if it had not enjoyed the acquiescence of the population in general and the cooper-

ation of some segment of it in particular. When one re-
calls the small numbers of Europeans who resided in the
colonies and administered them—a few hundred thousand Englishmen among several hundred million Indians, for instance—the need for such acquiescence and
support becomes obvious.

Under these circumstances the Europeans seldom
purposely jarred the existing social order. They certainly
manipulated political leaders, overlaid their own institutions on those of the local society, and began the process
of social change with the creation of modern urban complexes such as New Delhi and Casablanca.[9] And, of
course, they spawned a new elite both anxious to imitate
Western ways and soon desirous to eject the Westerner
himself. But the European overseas empires, it will be
recalled, were administrative empires, not consciously
designed instruments of social change and revolution.

As the new generation of colonial elites came into
their own political maturity and assessed the significance
of the forces of social change which were around them,
they rejected both of the pasts which still bound them
and seemed to account for the disadvantageous position
in which they found themselves. Not only was colonial
authority rejected, but also the prevalent indigenous social
order, that which had first been incapable of resisting the
Europeans and then had been compromised into serving
them, was denounced. The mandarins in Indochina, the

[9] A wealth of material on the transformation from the traditional to modern society presently exists. Two suggestive and
already classic accounts are: Daniel Lerner, *The Passing of
Traditional Society* (Glen Cove), 1958; and Lucien Pye, *Politics, Personality and Nation Building* (New Haven), 1961.

sultans in Indonesia, the tribal chiefs in parts of Africa, and even the reigning dynasties in Tunisia and Egypt gradually lost support. The colonial nationalist movements were generally republican. Their appeal was most frequently to social groups other than those currently in power.[10]

Most everywhere the Europeans were soon affected by the erosion of the foundations of their imperial authority. Both command and acquiescence, the twin pillars of imperialist strength, were weakened, in effect leaving the Europeans with but two alternatives, neither of which was pleasant to contemplate: (1) either attempted continuation of rule by means of forceful domination, reversion to police power; or (2) capitulation to the demands of the nationalists.

When the latter alternative was accepted in those countries where the national independence movements were the most vociferous and abrasive, as in India or Tunisia, the possibility of forestalling similar movements elsewhere was greatly limited. Nationalism can be called a social virus which infects and spreads very quickly. Once Asia and North Africa had reached a feverish condition, Africa south of the Sahara could not be expected to remain isolated for long. Sir Denis Brogan could write as late as 1951:

There remains one area where the old imperialism is not dead and where it may still have a good deal of life in it,

[10] A notable exception to this statement is the ruling house of Morocco. The French exile of the late Mohammed V in 1953 cast him in the role of a national leader resisting French imperialism.

barring war and a breakdown of authority comparable to that brought about by the Japanese victories in Asia. In Africa, the old order stands, though there, as everywhere else, it is threatened.[11]

Even in this cautious estimate, Brogan was too generous. Within ten years after he made this statement, African empire was gone and in its stead stood some two dozen new African states.

In really jig time, hardly more than fifteen years, powerful and extensive European colonial empires disintegrated into a wide variety and large number of nation-states. This quick transformation was primarily the work of the leaders of the aroused indigenous populations, not the results of European intentions or planning. Although frequently bantered about as a noble objective or a clearly defined goal, independence was neither seriously studied nor widely entertained by the colonial powers until the postwar era. Furthermore, the anticolonialism of the United States, Russia, and the United Nations would never have been enough to cause the collapse of colonial empire. The real credit must be given to the colonial peoples themselves. The following remark can be extended without seriously altering its original meaning:

The conventional phrase which speaks of the imperial power "granting" self-government is misleading; Canada, first, and

[11] Sir Denis Brogan, *The Price of Revolution* (New York, 1951), p. 146.

others later, were many years facing their difficulties for themselves and patiently working out a higher destiny.[12]

Most everywhere self-government was wrested from the colonial power or demanded with sufficient insistence that the colonial power was compelled to allow it. If the most recent ascendants to the level of nationalist independence have arrived there because the colonial powers offered no resistance and, indeed, offered encouragement, this outcome must be largely attributed to the determined efforts and militancy of those earlier nationalist movements which first budged the colonial powers. And yet the colonial powers also were usually wise enough—and weary enough—not to countenance resistance with harsher resistance. In the case of France, the futile and frightful war in Indochina and the equally unfortunate struggle in Algeria not only weakened but also toppled the government of the Fourth Republic. This is some indication of the economic and moral strain such resistance could have had elsewhere had it been undertaken.

The end of empire immediately satisfied neither party: the colonialist because he felt he had not been given enough time to realize his ideal plans; the colonized because he had not been given sufficient preparation. Even so, the postcolonial world is not characterized by universal or even general antagonism and resentment between the former colonizers and the former colonial peoples. Suspicion may reign, but so does a spirit of cooperation.

[12] William Macmillan, *The Road to Self-Rule* (London, 1959), p. 66.

6 . AFTER EMPIRE, WHAT?

The historical phenomenon of overseas empire is now all but over, and it can safely be stated that such an occurrence will not happen again. The constellation of political and economic factors which enabled Europe to expand most everywhere it pleased has disappeared from the contemporary horizon. For the first time in modern history Europe's political significance has been greatly reduced, if not to a size commensurate with its geographical boundaries, at least to the point where the world is no longer Eurocentric. By 1967 the states which wielded the most effective world power were the continental monoliths of America and Russia, huge land masses embracing large populations and containing ample natural resources.

This change, however, does not mean that the former colonies and dominions are free to enjoy unqualifiedly the pleasures of sovereign independence. The situation of Africa and Asia has not altered that much. Our contemporary world is still one in which wealth and power are highly concentrated in a few areas, sparingly distributed in most others. The rich nations are a handful, the poor nations a multitude. Even though France and England have declined relatively, they still rank high among the world's industrial powers, as part of that select group with elevated standards of living, impressive gross national products.

Although today no longer so clearly defined, the world in the last two decades has tended to be bifurcated politically with the rival superstates which profess antagonistic ideologies seeking to enlist the support of the uncommitted nations of Africa and Asia or striving to assure that these nations do not gravitate to the other side. While the policy of nonalignment has characterized the international stance of many of the African and Asian nations, the influence of the Cold War has had its effects on their politics. Military agreements and foreign aid both suggest the attached strings by which one side or the other has attempted to manipulate and to bind.

What perhaps most clearly distinguishes the postcolonial from the colonial world is this: the former gravitates toward the United States and Russia as well as to Western Europe, whereas the latter converged almost entirely on Western Europe. The essential point to be made here

is that a continuation of inequality and imbalance among
the regions and nations of the world is most evident.
Whatever the changes which have occurred since World
War II in the composition of international power and influence, they have not altered the fact that the Third
World still remains third: the revolution of expectations, both in its political and economic phases, has yet to
come. This state of affairs in which much of Asia and
Africa still seems to be dominated in some way or other
by the West, and even the East, has encouraged the formulation of a new neologism which pretends to discover
an old practice now hidden: neo-colonialism, or overseas
imperialism in new disguise.

Neo-colonialism is a charged word; it arouses emo-
tions as often as it provokes analysis. It is a workaday
word in the polemical arguments coming from the Third
World. President Sukarno, while he was riding high on
the crests of the political waves he generated in his "Indonesian" Ocean, employed the term almost as frequently
as he coined others. World leaders as diverse in political
temperament as Mao Tse-tung, Kwame Nkrumah, Joseph Nyerere, and Gamal Abdel Nasser have found many
occasions to use it. Only in the Western world has the
word appeared puzzling. Former British Prime Minister
Lord Hume once commented that he did not know it or
understand its meaning. This is perhaps understandable,
for it is a word which depends essentially on a perspective, that of the underdog, the underdeveloped nation.

As a generic term neo-colonialism includes most any
activity which the rich and powerful nations of the
world, and particularly the former colonial powers, now

undertake in Africa and Asia. The following explanation, provided by a British Communist political writer, suggests the enormous proportions the term can display:

Neo-colonialism includes not only economic domination, but also all kinds of political and military means to maintain or restore domination after the granting of formal sovereign independence to a former colony. Neo-colonialism includes the imposition of partition or twisted constitutions to maintain reactionary collaborators with imperialism in power after the recognition of independence. Neo-colonialism includes the maintenance of imperialist military bases in the territory of the newly independent country. Neo-colonialism includes entanglement in imperialist military alliances like CENTO or SEATO, or even direct military intervention to restore an overthrown hated dictator, as by French imperialism in Gabon, or to destroy an elected parliamentary majority and majority Premier and establish military gangster rule, as in the Congo, or as practiced wholesale by the United States imperialism in Latin America and Eastern Asia, and by British imperialism in South-East Asia and the Middle East.[1]

Here compounded are old and familiar ingredients: capitalist exploitation, balance of power, gunboat diplomacy, puppet rule, the principle of divide and conquer. There is nothing connected with the old imperialism and colonialism which this particular definition ignores.

From such a snarl of fact and fancy, we must seek the main strands of neo-colonialism, those arguments and facts which give it its strength and pattern. First, an

[1] R. Palme Dutt, "British Colonial Policy and Neo-Colonial Rivalries," *International Affairs* (Moscow), November 8, 1964, p. 35.

appreciation of the term as employed by its protagonists; then an attempt at dispassionate historical judgment.

If it has any authentic parentage, neo-colonialism comes out of the economic interpretation of imperialism, most specifically the Leninist one. It should be recalled that imperialism was therein considered a stage in capitalist development and a device by which the capitalists maintained and augmented their profits through the exploitation of the backward regions of the world. Yet despite the analysis and prediction provided by Lenin this highest or last stage of capitalistic development has not yet been followed by the collapse or overthrow of the West's prevalent economic-political system. Today, interpreters in the Marxist-Leninist tradition find no fault with Lenin's analysis but attribute the continuation of capitalism to the use of new imperialistic methods. Neo-colonialism, or imperialism without empire, is considered to be the most significant of these.

The old objectives are still relentlessly pursued, but now the operations transpire behind the façade of nominally sovereign states and with the cooperation or acquiescence of ruling elites and local bourgeois classes. Neo-colonialism is, or has been considered to be, synonymous with what some historians have called the "informal" empire first established by Great Britain in Latin America in the early nineteenth century and then enlarged upon by the United States in the heyday of dollar diplomacy. The First African, Asian, and Latin American Peoples' Solidarity Conference, directed primarily against "Yankee Imperialism" and appropriately sitting in Havana in January 1966, stated in its resolution on colonialism and neo-colonialism:

The first victims of this neo-colonialist policy were the Latin American countries which, after almost all having conquered their political independence in the last century, found themselves submitted to the economic penetration first of British imperialism—and, to a lesser degree, French imperialism—and then principally to North American imperialism.

This statement can be complemented with one which has an official Russian Communist ring, that offered by L. Goncharov, Member of the African Institute of the U.S.S.R. Academy of Sciences:

The colonial powers . . . are striving to find at least a partial substitute for the direct political control which is slipping out of their hands, in order to retain their main function, economic exploitation. . . . New forms of colonialism simply represent the strategy and tactics of retreating imperialism. Neo-colonialism is spearheaded against countries which are gaining or have already gained political sovereignty.[2]

As indicated in this assessment, neo-colonialism is imperialism on the defensive in a world hostile to it. Faced with the disappearance of old-style colonial empire, with ever more powerful and successful national liberation movements, and with the emergence of a socialist world united in its opposition to all forms of Western control, the imperialists can no longer employ their old devices. One sign of this weakness has been the substitution of

[2] L. Goncharov, "New Forms of Colonialism in Africa," *Journal of Modern African Studies*, I, 4 (1963), p. 467.

collective or international efforts for the separate national actions characteristic of pre-World War II European imperialism. NATO, SEATO, the Common Market—particularly as it is related to Africa—are offered as proof of this decline; they represent combinations born of fear, not of strength and confidence.

Yet this is not all. Changes in the contemporary economic order of things have also had their effects. Noting that private investment in a region such as Africa has tapered off in the last few years while private investment from outside, notably from the United States, has increased in many European countries, some Marxist writers have concluded that the nature of contemporary industrialism demands that the greatest capitalist investment be made in the more developed industrial regions because of the complicated and sophisticated nature of present-day production techniques. There is therefore no longer any question of exploiting the cheap but ill-trained labor available in the poorer countries. Instead the chief capitalist objective in these countries has become control of their commerce. This is achieved not only by means of direct, long-distance exportation of products but also by means of their local distribution through the use of regional assembly plants belonging to the foreign corporation and also through the sale of licenses for local manufacture of certain products. The spread of Coca-Cola sales from corner drugstore to pyramid and palm tree has many times been cited as an obvious example of foreign economic domination by American corporate interests.

The conclusion to be drawn from the arguments just

presented is an obvious one: if, as a result of decolonization, the instruments and devices of capitalist imperialism have changed, and, if as a result of growing opposition, this imperialism is everywhere threatened, its
ultimate purposes have not changed at all since Lenin's
appraisal of them: domination and exploitation of the
many for the sake of profits for the few.

Here is "empire," the empire of financial capital, in fact, if
not in name, a vast sprawling network of intercontinental
activity on a highly diversified scale that controls the lives of
millions of people in the most widely separated parts of the
world, manipulating whole industries and exploiting the
labour and the riches of nations for the greedy satisfaction
of a few. . . .

This is the description of neo-colonialism offered by former President Nkrumah of Ghana.[3]

The result of such contemporary interpretations of
neo-colonialist imperialism has been that the older
Marxist-Leninist thesis has lost none of its relevancy
and has, moreover, acquired new popularity. Most of
the theorists and political leaders in the so-called socialist
camp of the underdeveloped world—running from Cas-
tro in Cuba eastward around the globe to Mao in China
—have employed this thesis as the explanation of their
opposition to the capitalist West and, most particularly,
to the United States, its chief representative. While its
scientific value may be minimal or nil, the ideological
value of the Marxist-Leninist thesis cannot be dis-

[3] Kwame Nkrumah, *Neo-Colonialism the Last Stage of Imperialism* (London, 1965), pp. 35–36.

counted, for this thesis gathers appeal as it continues to provide that awesome symmetry which is characteristic of reductionist interpretations of complex historical developments.

The economic aspects of the neo-colonialist argument need not and do not always rest on a rigid Marxist-Leninist basis, however. Some writers describe the problem as economic domination, whatever the intention or lack thereof, by wealthy and powerful nations, regardless of their political or economic persuasion. In their eyes, any form of economic dependence makes political independence, hence internal freedom, only nominal. In the words of Mamoudou Dia, former premier of Senegal: "A certain number of recently emancipated states have understood perfectly well that sovereignty in this world is only real when carried out technically, economically." [4]

The economic argument takes on further ramifications when the political rivalries and seeming machinations of the great states are also included. Britain's creation of Malaysia has been labeled neo-colonialist; Belgium's support of Moise Tshombe's Katanga secessionist movement has also been so stamped; and so has French military intervention in Gabon. Even Russia has not been excluded. Again, from Mamoudou Dia: "The Soviet offensive in the underdeveloped countries, the menace of the Cold War, illustrate well this new evolution toward an economic colonialism."

American foreign policy, however, has received the most extensive neo-colonialist denunciation. As the

---

[4] Mamoudou Dia, *Nations africaines et solidarité mondiale* (Paris, 1960), p. 40.

United States has rushed in where the former colonial powers have pulled out, it appears to be replacing them in function and purpose. American interference in Vietnam, Lebanon, the Congo, even the Dominican Republic, has been seen as part of an emerging neo-colonialist pattern. Added to this direct political and military action are such institutions and efforts as the treaty organizations—NATO, SEATO, CENTO—foreign aid, and even the Peace Corps. Again turning to Nkrumah for a forceful presentation of the argument, here is the American role assessed:

Foremost among the neo-colonialists is the United States, which has long exercised its power in Latin America. Fumbling at first she turned toward Europe, and then with more certainty after world war two when most countries of that continent were indebted to her. Since then, with methodical thoroughness and touching attention to detail, the Pentagon set about consolidating its ascendency, evidence of which can be seen all around the world.[5]

To this list of active neo-colonialist nations could be added West Germany, Israel, and Japan, and to the list of neo-colonialist devices could be added Western education, literature and languages, and cultural exchanges. Indeed, all of these have been itemized in the general catalogue.

There is no doubt that neo-colonialism has been recklessly used and ill-defined, but it is not a term without purpose. It clearly represents an attitude, that of suspicion on the part of the former colonial peoples who have

[5] Nkrumah, *loc. cit.*, p. 239.

yet too little reason to accept the contemporary actions of the rich and powerful nations of the world as being radically different in intention from those earlier expressed. Moreover, the term has its ideological uses. If we return to the discussion of colonial nationalism momentarily, we recall that imperialism performed the service of accounting for all the major disadvantages which the colonized regions of the world found facing them. Neo-colonialism provides much the same service in the period of national independence when many of these disadvantages still persist and perplex contemporary governments. Among other things, neo-colonialism is something of a useful bogey man.

None of this is meant to dismiss out of hand the neo-colonialism argument; rather it is intended to explain from whence it derives its force and its appeal. What still has to be considered are the real foundations of neo-colonialism, both economic and political.

One small portion of the world still dominates the great masses of land and peoples who are far removed from it. Commercial goods, military arms, capital, technicians, and technical advice flow from the rich to the poor regions all the while seeming to be no drain on the former and little stimulant to the latter. To provide a contemporary twist to Marx's dictum that the rich get richer and the poor get poorer, one could say that today the rich nations get richer while the poor nations remain poor.

This world imbalance is rather easily accounted for. The "take-off" of the Western nations to modern industrialism occurred much earlier than elsewhere, thus giving the West an initial advantage which it has held on to quite well. In the imperialist age the colonial regions provided many of the raw materials which made the factories of Europe run and also provided some of the markets which absorbed the finished products. Whatever the motives, the West tied the rest of the world to it by its lines of trade and finance. In the post-World War II era, there has been little serious alteration of this arrangement, with the notable exception of the dominant role played by the United States of America, which now consumes half of the world's raw materials and dominates an impressive amount of the world's markets.

In effect, the economic dependency of the Third World, created before the end of imperialism, continues and has increased. A quick review of the major factors involved in this dependency may be in order. (1) The self-sufficient or self-centered local and regional economies of most underdeveloped countries in the precolonial age were disrupted and replaced by vastly extended markets: the Kenyan Highlands, the Mekong Delta, and the Congo jungles were absorbed into an international system from which retreat would now be difficult, if not disastrous. In short, colonial economies became export economies, susceptible to the oscillations of the exterior market and directed to the particular needs of industrial Europe. (2) With the creation of infrastructures designed to serve European economic and administrative requirements, the colonial regions increased their dependency on rather sophisticated and complex technical services for which they had too few well-trained members of their own cultures. The Europeans generally retained the key positions in this complex for themselves and did little to train the indigenous populations to assume them. (3) In the present period of national independence, the Third World is intent upon its modernization, which implies both the increase and improvement of agricultural and industrial production. The non-Western world enters modernity at that point of history where highly refined electronic and automated devices regulate industry and where agriculture is mechanically organized and chemically enriched. This is the age of the jet aircraft, the computer, and the gasoline tractor, not that of the steam engine, the double-entry ledger, and the dray horse. What is obviously needed is not sheer numbers of people ("hands" in nineteenth-century parlance) but well-trained professional and semiprofessional personnel. Given the rudimentary or insufficient state of educational systems bequeathed them, these new nations are not yet in a position to supply all of their own needs. While the process of replacement of Europeans has recently increased—the "Africanization" of cadres, for instance—Americans, Frenchmen, Englishmen, Belgians, and Russians still are to be found at many of the centers of things. (4) Moreover, the equipment used for the preparatory stages of modernization comes essentially from the rich nations of the West. Ford tractors, English Land-Rovers, Krupp-built extractors, and French Berliet trucks are but the most visible daily signs of this condition. A glance at the advertisements of any internationally oriented magazine will suggest the multitudinous activities and extended involvement of the West in the underdeveloped world. One last factor bears mentioning: much of the capital made available for financing these enterprises comes from the West. Put most briefly, colonial dependency meant economic dependency; national independence still means economic dependency.

The argument that the division of labor in the world has been made and enforced by the former colonial powers, now joined and indeed surpassed by the United States, has its appeal: is not the underdeveloped world still agrarian and unmodernized? And is not the West the principal industrial and modernized area of the world? Does not the latter's privileged position then depend on the former's underprivileged condition?

To select one example which suggests this asymmetrical relationship and one which has often been used to illustrate the neo-colonialist argument, let us turn to the association of eighteen African states with the European Economic Community, generally known as the Common Market. Earlier affiliated with the Community as colonies, principally of France, these new African states were invited by the Community to join in the establishment of new economic arrangements. Discussions finally resulted in a treaty signed at Yaoundé in the Cameroons in July 1963, a treaty which was designed to create a vast Eurafrican economic area in which goods, services, and capital could flow freely. The European states were to reduce progressively both tariff and quantitative restrictions on products coming from the African states. These states were in turn to cease existing tariff discrimination so that all of the six European states would be treated equally, and they were also to reduce progressively tariff and quantitative restrictions on goods originating from the Six. Moreover, the Six were to help stimulate African economic activity both by private investment and by public development funds. Finally, safeguard clauses were inserted in the treaty to allow the separate African states to make those economic adjustments they considered necessary for their individual development. However, approval of such adjustments was only to be made by the Council of the Association consisting of representatives of all twenty-four states. An official publication of the Community stated that "the essential objective of the association is the economic and social development of the African states."

Critics have seen its purpose in no such light. To them the association is a form of neo-colonialism, a means by which the former European colonial powers, most particularly France, can continue to enjoy a privileged position in much of Africa. As designed, they contend, the association provides the six capitalist European states with ready and unhindered access to both the markets and the raw materials of the African states. It thus tends to perpetuate the division of labor in the world, mentioned earlier, with the more powerful and already industrialized European states increasing and dumping their industrial production on these African countries, which, as a result, will be kept in an agrarian, hence subordinate, economic position. By requiring that adjustments made to accommodate the economic needs of the individual states be approved by the Council of the Association, in which all twenty-four states participate, the agreement tends to hinder, if not prevent, individual economic development. Finally, European capital would have an open field for financial investment. It is for these reasons that the association has been denounced as collective imperialism, as neo-colonialism, as a contemporary version of the old colonial pact.

Lest the Europeans alone be here scrutinized, let us turn to the American economic position vis-à-vis Africa. If this country exhibited little interest or desire to invest in Africa or to utilize its raw materials before the last war (Firestone's rubber interests in Liberia excepted), the opposite attitude now seems to have developed. By 1961 imports from Africa had increased sixfold, exports eightfold, and investments sevenfold. Compared with economic activity at home and elsewhere abroad, American involvement in Africa only yields small percentages— four per cent of total American exports, two per cent of total American investment abroad in 1961—but they are suggestive of a trend. "The real direct economic interest of the United States in Africa is in the future. Africa as a source of raw materials and as a market for United States goods is destined to play a more important part in the American economy in the future." [6] Could not this statement be easily rephrased in mercantilist terms, and could it not easily be interpreted as being expressive of neo-colonialism?

The truth is, whether there be chicanery afoot or not, the Western dominance of the underdeveloped world has

[6] Andrew M. Kamarck, "The African Economy and International Trade," in Walter Goldschmidt, ed., *The United States and Africa* (New York), 1963, p. 159. The preceding statistics also came from this article.

increased, and concomitantly so has the economic subservience of the underdeveloped world.

To make sense of it all, however, is not an easy task, but one of the clearest and most satisfactory attempts is that offered by the Swedish author, Gunnar Myrdal, in his slim volume, *Economic Theory and Under-Developed Regions.*[7] Myrdal's argument hinges upon a principle he calls "circular causation of cumulative development." This Myrdal explains quite effectively by the use of a biblical quotation: "For unto every one that hath shall be given, and he shall have abundance; but from him that hath not shall be taken even that which he hath." In Marx's terms again, the rich get richer, the poor get poorer. Those states which obtained initial advantages tend not only to keep them but to accumulate more. The initially disadvantaged states continue to remain in that dismal condition.

Myrdal argues that in economic development equilibrium does not obtain, nor is there any tendency in that direction. On the contrary, imbalance persists. Where a major change occurs, there is seldom a countervailing change to balance it, but rather other changes which support and reinforce it. Left unchecked by controls, such as those provided by government, the economic condition will tend to cumulate upward for some regions and states, downward for others, as one change after another adds to the respective development or decline. The most striking example of an upward spiral would be the

[7] Gunnar Myrdal, *Economic Theory and Under-Developed Regions* (London, 1957). The significant chapters are 2 and 5.

United States, where industrial power has meant higher standards of living, better health, and better educational systems, which in turn have meant better-trained workers, an impetus to the development of new industries and an increase in domestic markets, all of this further enriching the country industrially and monetarily. The standard example of the downward spiral—and one that Myrdal employs—is the underdeveloped region where people are poor and unhealthy because their economic standards and capacity are low, this poverty-stricken condition in turn assuring that economic development will be a near impossibility and hence stagnation will continue.

Somewhat as if operating on a principle of cultural or social inertia, the rich regions move ahead, while the poor ones tend to stand still or to retreat. To return to Myrdal and his own terms again, within the process of cumulative development there are "spread effects"; the extension of economic and social advantages to neighboring regions as the center of industrial development produces a centrifugal force. And there are also "backwash effects," the draining and the stagnation of certain economic and social resources of initially poorer or disadvantaged regions as a result of the centripetal force of industrial development elsewhere. Thus the industrial north of Italy and the United States enjoyed "spread effects"; the south of both regions suffered from "backwash effects."

If transferred to the colonial and postcolonial situation, Myrdal's theory provides a coherent explanation of the phenomenon of economic dominance discussed earlier. It is the colonial powers that have enjoyed the best of circular causation; the colonies which have generally suffered from the accumulation of adversities. And viewed internationally, the "spread effects" have occurred in the colonial nations; the "backwash effects" in the colonies. What this has meant is an asymmetrical economic relationship, one aggravated by "enforced bilateralism," the administrative and institutional links which the colonizing power has forged with its colonies.

As Myrdal and others have insisted, this economic condition need not be the natural order of things, for such development will continue primarily if left uncontrolled, that is, if left to the vagaries of market forces. Thus, even if Western economic dominance of much of the world is more the result of circumstance than of conspiracy, many critics have rightly raised the question: what are the rich nations, and notably the United States, doing to help correct this disparity, to help equalize the difference between the rich and the poor? It is within the context of this question that the neo-colonialist argument gathers significance.

Any glance at statistics will show that since the end of World War II Europe and the United States have provided the underdeveloped world with much assistance, both in the form of private investment and public aid. But an analysis of the purposes to which this assistance has been turned would suggest that it has done all too little to assure the economic betterment desired in these new countries.

Private investment has been more beneficial to the investor than to the country in which it has been invested.

Considerable profits return to the metropolitan country; high company officials on the local payroll are often Western nationals whose salaries will be spent chiefly at home; equipment for the local enterprise most often comes from metropolitan industry. Although most underdeveloped countries now have precise laws regulating the sharing of profits between foreign investor and national government, the former has not been adversely affected by these to the point where he finds his activities unprofitable.

Of course the private corporation is not a philanthropic organization by definition. It should, however, be pointed out that the investment made in the underdeveloped country does have its local benefits. The plant and much of the equipment become part of that country's industrial establishment; new sources of employment are provided for an underemployed population; on-the-job training increases the efficiency and quality of local labor; accumulated profits flow in part to the local government. Yet critics still argue that the foreign company is a drain through which natural resources and accumulated capital are forced out of the country. The early history of British and American oil companies in the Middle East and American oil companies in Latin America lends credence to this argument.

Foreign aid emanating from public sources is certainly not profit-directed, but it has too often gone abroad "attached." It should be recalled that the greatest amount of such aid has been for military purposes, not for the social and economic betterment of resident populations. Unfortunately, some of the aid not earmarked for military purposes has been squandered on projects with little economic viability—palaces and airlines, for instance— and much has been too carelessly dispersed over a variety of projects to have appreciable effect on the process of modernization. Where such aid has been constructively used, as in the building of hydroelectric dams, port and railroad facilities, or factories, it is true that local industrialization has been stimulated. However, even here the critics have a final word.

In their policy of foreign aid the nations of the West, and again the United States principally, have tended to give their greatest support to those underdeveloped nations whose political affiliation or sympathy was the most assured. Frequently, these nations have been ruled by regimes which are oligarchic in organization, undemocratic in practice, and conservative in outlook. Criticism centers on the contention that foreign aid has thus tended at times to perpetuate the old order, one at times out of tune with the needs and desires of its population. The Vietnam of Diem, the Formosa of Chiang, the Jordan of King Hussein have all been cited as examples.

One of the reasons for which foreign aid and investment have not fully realized the expectations of the underdeveloped nations has been the narrow or restricted purposes for which this support has been granted. If the rich nations of the world, both East and West, replaced a national with an international vision—a sense of genuine philanthropy, to be idealistic about it—the general imbalance in the world today might be better corrected, the results socially beneficial. Instead of national competition with an emphasis on arms build-up, a well-coordinated and well-planned international aid program might be introduced, with capital, services, and equipment moving in the underdeveloped world under international control and unaccompanied by previously determined economic and political qualifications beneficial first and foremost to the donor nation.

Yet the detriment to the realization of a cumulative spiral upward in the underdeveloped world comes also from a complex of problems which are found within. Despite the efforts of the new nationalistically inclined elites to make the "great leap forward," there remain strong forces within the land which hold back and weigh down.

These may be grouped together in the homely phrase: the old way of life. Remember that the era of imperialist rule was not one of widely extended innovation or planned social revolution. The European presence, both personally and institutionally, had a disturbing effect on local society, it is true, but that society still had its many isolated regions in bush and savanna, on the plains and in the jungles, where European rule and civilization hardly penetrated at all. Away from the urban and administrative centers from which radiated European power, the peasant continued to plow the fields of his narrow domain; the witch doctor and the midwife practiced their ancient and insufficient skills; the mother fed her child by instinct, not from knowledge of nutrition. It was all still a familial and familiar world, seemingly repetitious from one generation to the next. Of course, traditional societies were not static, and they were shaken into motion by European imperialism. But even at the end of the imperialist era they were still not prepared to enter modernity on their own without considerable travail.

To create modern societies where traditional cultures stood before is the essential task confronting the present ruling elites, and to do this they must turn inward to disturb and disrupt the old order. What this means is that the stimulus which Western rule gave to a small number of the indigenous population has now to be transferred to the masses.

The new governments and administrations are attempting to destroy and create at one time: to detribalize, deruralize, demystify; and to reorganize socially and economically. Such an enormous task requires much money, able bureaucrats, and also some ideal or principle by which to mobilize opinion and hence to direct action: in a word, an ideology. It has been to socialism that most of the emerging nations have turned, but not necessarily Marxian socialism. While variously defined, the socialism of these nations implies first and foremost government control—but not ownership—for the purpose of improving and rationalizing the economy; this means national planning and extensive training. But secondly socialism is seen as a spiritual force, an ideal and an attitude by which to bind the people into a common cause. As President Leopold Senghor once stated:

But it is not only a question of training "able minds" and skilled technicians—from the worker and the farmer to the engineer. It is rather a matter of training conscientious citizens with a taste for work well done and for creative innovation; above all men with a common sense of interest.[8]

[8] A speech of January 25, 1963, cited in *Africa Report*, VIII, 5 (May 1963), p. 24.

Nor can anyone really dispute the value of the socialist ideal. The multitudinous problems—capital formation, creation of administrative cadres, education of a lethargic population, establishment of basic industries, development of scientific agriculture—demand more than a laissez-faire government. The regions of the Third World enter nationhood at that time in history when the functions of the state extend far beyond those of the nineteenth century summed up in Ferdinand Lassalle's apt phrase "the night watchman state." Of social necessity, the state is now more positive, more welfare-conscious. These responsibilities which the new states wish to assume compound the difficulties arising from general modernization. And, moreover, there is no powerful economic middle class or extensive private capital reserves to be encouraged toward assistance in the task outlined. As a result, there is little opportunity for the new states to practice the old dictum: pull yourselves up by your own bootstraps.

Because of this, and despite their pronouncements about socialism, most of the new nations realize full well the need for foreign investment and aid as a source of necessary capital and equipment. Yet from the "down under" point of view policies of foreign aid and investment are risky.

The problem therefore is how to obtain capital investment and still to keep it under sufficient control to prevent undue exploitation and how to preserve integrity and sovereignty without crippling economic or political ties to any country, bloc or system.

These words of Kwame Nkrumah,[9] one of the most forceful exponents of the idea of neo-colonialism, suggest the perhaps necessary ambivalence of the new nations: their desire for and fear of foreign assistance.

This condition of economic dependency, which is at the root of the neo-colonialist argument, will not be seriously altered for some time to come. In one form or another the richer nations which have enjoyed an edge in development will no doubt remain dominant. Yet such a situation is not new in history. Indeed, a history of world economics could be written around the theme of dominating and dominated economies.[10] Rome, Venice, the Hanseatic League, and Holland have all preceded with some degree of success the handful of nations which now control, for better or for worse, the world markets.

The present inequities in the global economic order are no doubt more the result of what the French call the *force des choses* than of calculated mischief. Put otherwise, it is Myrdal, not Lenin, who offers the better explanation of this occurrence. But to say this, and hence to minimize any capitalistic "plot" thesis of the recent history of Africa and Asia, does not make an assessment of contemporary economic dependency any more pleasant, nor does it allow the smug conclusion that the rich nations are operating on noble principles and to the best of their financial ability. The economic interpretation of neo-colonialism does have the value of demonstrating

[9] A speech of February 22, 1963, cited in *ibid.*, pp. 30–31.
[10] On this subject see François Perroux, *L'Economie du XXeme Siècle* (Paris, 1961).

how little these nations have done for the social welfare and general economic betterment of the populations in the underdeveloped world. Not until international responsibility replaces national self-interest, no matter how enlightened, will the accusations of "capitalist duplicity" and of "crass exploitation" found in the more hyperstated forms of neo-colonialist arguments be completely emptied of any meaning.

If the issue of self-interest were essentially one of private profit, its removal or adjustment might be easily managed, but contemporary world economics are still too frequently subordinated to world politics. The present world situation has led the new nations of the Third World to serious international involvement at the very moment they acquire their nationhood and the domestic problems that it entails. Economic aid and assistance have meant political affiliation on more than one occasion, as East and West have sought to dominate by donation. In this area of international activity, the neo-colonialist argument has further significance.

The international political order which arose from the ashes of World War II was not like the Phoenix, a splendid thing to behold. Initial hopes for one world based on respect for the rights of self-determination were soon shattered, as the wartime Grand Alliance fell apart into opposing camps. The resulting political situation was characterized by what has been called bipolarization: two poles of political attraction—the United States and the Soviet Union—and the states which gravitated to one or the other. While the rivalry and antagonism of the two superstates first centered in Europe, it soon spread around the world as the Cold War crystallized world affairs and even reached—in defiance of the metaphor—combustion temperatures in Korea in 1950. The East-West struggle thus complicated the process of decolonization and nation-building and caused concern and anxiety to be expressed by many African and Asian governments.

The history of the Cold War is a familiar one and therefore need only be recalled here in its broad terms. It began on the morrow of the Allied victory in World War II when the expansionism of Stalinist Russia became a serious concern to the American government. Russia moved initially and without hesitation into the regions she traditionally coveted: Eastern Europe and the Near East. Not only had she made early inroads in the Baltic area thanks to the Non-Aggression Pact she had concluded with Nazi Germany in 1939, but also she profited from the later war situation. As the Nazis were pushed back, the Soviets simply absorbed these regions but a bit earlier brutally joined to the Third Reich. Puppet regimes were established in Poland, Hungary, Bulgaria, and Albania; Yugoslavia went Communist, and—until 1948 and Marshal Tito's assertion of his national independence—was part of the Communist bloc.

In the Near East similar moves were made. Russia and her satellites, notably Yugoslavia, gave aid to the Communist guerrillas fighting against the conservative Greek government in 1946. An autonomous republic was set up in Iranian Azerbaijan, after a contrived revolution, and was momentarily guaranteed by the presence of Soviet military forces. Finally, Turkey felt Soviet pressure as the Russians demanded joint Russo-Turkish bases in the Straits area and also some territorial concessions.

In face of what was outright continental imperialism, the government of the United States forcefully responded. In the spring of 1946 President Truman enunciated his Truman Doctrine in which he gave military and economic support to Greece and Turkey and thus gave notice to Russia that the United States intended to allow it no easy hand in the regulation of world affairs. In June of 1947 Secretary of State George Marshall in his now-famous speech at Harvard University outlined an American plan for assistance to war-torn Europe and stated that the United States would do whatever was possible "to assist in the return of normal economic health in the world, without which there can be no political stability and no assured peace." Then, in 1949, the United States helped reorganize the military defenses of Europe with the institution of the North Atlantic Treaty Organization.

These decisive political, economic, and military actions were attempts on the part of the American government to check Russian expansion. Indeed "containment" became official policy, complete with political and philosophical justification. But containment was not limited to the notion of holding back; it also included the policy of building up. Acting upon the assumption that Communism was chiefly a threat to those nations and regions which were economically and militarily weak, the United States government began the largest and most generous foreign aid policy history has recorded.

A good case can be made for the magnanimity and idealism of the United States in her assistance, but there is also the easy tendency to exaggerate the role played by humanitarianism or philanthropy in any nation's foreign policy. The first principle of foreign policy must be the assurance of a nation's security, and the United States recognizes this as such. Whereas isolationism seemed a satisfactory way of answering this need in an earlier age, the opposite is true today. Involvement is the price paid by a rich and powerful state which, through two world wars and its own economic development, has found itself thrust onto the center stage of the contemporary political drama.

What the United States really formulated was a policy of enlightened self-interest, of helping herself by helping other states. National concerns now extended globally, with the troubled areas in which friendly, if beleaguered, governments existed receiving the most attention and assistance. This assistance took the form of dollar grants both for military defense and economic improvement. Western Europe received the lion's share, with the Near East and Asia coming next. Greece, Japan, Nationalist China, and Korea were the outstanding non-European recipients. Latin America and Africa each received less money between 1945 and 1956 than did Greece, no doubt because they had no high political priority at the time.

Despite the idealism professed by the American government in its foreign policy, the alignment of nations on the side of the West was not unalloyed. Portugal, Spain, China-Taiwan, Vietnam of Ngo Dinh Diem, Batista's

Cuba hardly qualified as democracies and "freely governed" peoples. To many observers the inclusion of such states indicated that American foreign policy was based primarily on profound fear of Communism and not on the principles of democratic self-determination. With the moralistic stance assumed by Secretary of State Dulles during the Eisenhower administration, the American position stood out even more sharply. Then, the principle of neutrality, to which many of the Asian and African nations were attempting to adhere, was denounced. This principle, the Secretary of State affirmed in Iowa on June 9, 1956, "pretends that a nation can best gain safety for itself by being indifferent to the fate of others. This has become an obsolete conception, and, except under very exceptional circumstances, it is an immoral and short-sighted conception." As further confirmation of the rather rigid attitude assumed by the United States at this time, the Eisenhower administration cut off aid to Ceylon after it had negotiated a trade agreement with the Soviet Union.

From the "down under" perspective the attempts at a *pax americana* were not particularly inviting and suggested that in her endeavor to solicit support the United States was rushing in where the colonial powers were retreating. The power vacuum left by Great Britain in the Near East was quickly filled by the United States; Indochina, at least that portion now called Vietnam, was taken over from the French; American opposition to Lumumba and support to the more conservative regime of President Kasavubu in the Congo seemed to indicate that America was taking over somewhat from Belgium.

And, of course, the acquisition of island bases in the Pacific islands formerly belonging to Japan could be interpreted as the beginnings of a Pacific Empire. Last, and not the least aggravating, was the presence of American airforce bases in places like Morocco, Iran, and Thailand.

This complex of developments, perfectly comprehensible and honorable in the eyes of the American government, appeared shady to much of the Third World and soon led to the accusation of American imperialism and neo-colonialism, a theme which the Soviet Union and Communist China have repeated with endless monotony.

The Soviet Union was not left uncriticized, however. At the Bandung Conference of 1955, which many assumed would take a strong anti-American attitude, Sir John Kotelawala, Prime Minister of Ceylon, argued:

Colonialism is in many forms. The first and most obvious form is Western colonialism. . . . There is another form, however, about which many of us represented here are perhaps less clear in our minds and to which some of us would perhaps not agree to apply the term "colonialism" at all. Think for example of those satellite states under Communist domination in Central and Eastern Europe. . . . And if we are united in our opposition to colonialism, should it not be our duty openly to declare ourselves in opposition to Soviet colonialism as much as to Western colonialism?

Nine of the attending states agreed with this idea and condemned both Eastern and Western colonialism. On other occasions similar thoughts were expressed. From Senegal, as was mentioned earlier, Mamoudou Dia warned that Russian neo-colonialism was every bit as much to be feared as American. And Julius Neyere also cautioned about the extent of the neo-colonialist threat:

I believe that the socialist countries themselves, considered as "individuals" in the larger society of nations, are now committing the same crime committed by the capitalists before them. I believe that, on the international level, they are beginning to use wealth for the purpose of acquiring power and prestige.[11]

The fears expressed by governments in the Third World are not without foundation. Both the United States and the Soviet Union are doing their best to influence domestic and foreign affairs. While the Soviets crudely used military power in Eastern Europe under Stalin, the post-Stalinist age has been one in which the economic devices employed by the United States have also been employed by the Soviet Union. It is true that as the years progress down to the present, the strings of this economic aid have frequently been so loosely tied that it is often difficult to see how aid is attached to politics. Russian aid to India has not won that state over, nor did American aid to Nkrumah's Ghana convince that state to moderate its denunciations of American imperialism. But the rather unqualified aid currently granted many nations of the world is not an indication that Soviet-American relations have so warmed that the politics of the Cold War have evaporated. The abrasive Near Eastern situation, exploded by the Arab-Israeli War, is in part the result of Soviet-American power rivalry and

[11] A speech of August 5, 1961, cited in *Africa Report*, VIII, 5 (May 1963), pp. 22–23.

support there. On another continent the United States has defended its participation in the Vietnamese war in anti-Communist ideological terms. Finally, with the present activity of Communist China in parts of the Third World, the older duel is becoming more a tripartite struggle for influence and client states. In such a charged atmosphere accusations of imperialism and neocolonialism continue to flourish.

The Afro-Asian nations, however, have not been idly or passively watching the struggle of the giants. On the contrary, they have taken cognizance of their situation, a common one deriving from their former colonial status and contemporary underdeveloped condition, and have attempted to bring joint pressure to bear on world affairs.

The beginning of this new international attitude was the Bandung Conference of 1955. "Bandung was, in a manner of speaking, a historical pageant, symbolizing the coming of age of Asia and Africa." So wrote General Carlos Romulo of the Philippines, and his statement has been frequently paraphrased ever since. This conference to which twenty-nine of the nations of Africa and Asia were invited was the inspiration of the Colombo powers, Ceylon, Pakistan, Indonesia, and India, which were seriously concerned about the state of international affairs and the role possibly to be played by themselves. The purpose of the conference was clearly stated by Chou En Lai, foreign minister of Communist China: "The epoch when the Western powers controlled our destinies is over. The peoples of Asia and Africa must now guide their own destinies."

Although several of the Western states looked upon Bandung with trepidation—the United States foremost among them—because of possible anti-Western attitudes, the Conference was not severe in its attitude toward the West as such, nor was there any unanimous opinion in favor of neutralism. The most united and severe sentiment was that against colonialism, but there was also complete accord on such matters as nuclear disarmament, reduction of world tensions, and greater economic and cultural cooperation.

Bandung was the first expression of the nations of the Third World, a common chorus of hope and aspiration, of intention to assume responsible positions in world affairs. It was also an affirmation of a new and anticolonial sentiment, the "death of an inferiority complex," to quote Leopold Sedar Senghor.

In the next few years similar international conferences were held in Cairo, Conakry, and Belgrade, but none achieved either the enthusiasm or noble intentions characteristic of Bandung. Each, however, repeated familiar themes: anticolonialism, Afro-Asian cooperation, disarmament, relief from world tensions. The neutralist sentiment did grow, however. Speaking at the Belgrade Conference on September 2, 1961, Prime Minister Nehru defined this international political attitude:

We call ourselves a Conference of Non-Aligned Countries. Now the word non-aligned may be differently interpreted, but basically it was used and coined with the meaning non-aligned with the great power blocs of the world. Non-aligned has a negative meaning, but if you give it a positive connotation it means Nations which object to this lining-up for war purposes, military blocs, military alliances and the like. Therefore we keep away from this and we want to throw our weight, such as it is, in favor of peace.

What the Afro-Asian nations hoped to do was form a "bloc" to weigh against East and West, to become something of a third force in the world. This result was never achieved, and, indeed, as more African colonies reached nationhood, the term Afro-Asian became less frequently used, with an African bloc coming into existence. However, within the United Nations, the nations from the Third World were now sufficient in number—over eighty out of one hundred twenty-one—to make the General Assembly their forum and to check legislation which they deemed unfavorable to their own interests.

The efforts of the African and Asian states have hardly altered the world situation, however. International politics is still a game for the big states, and only a handful can play well at it. But no major state can afford to ignore or callously dismiss the opinions of such states. In this sense there is greater world responsibility as the great powers must now act with some caution and some consideration. Again, to quote Nehru at Belgrade:

We must not imagine that we can order about great countries, or as small countries do as we like. . . . but we have a certain capacity, a certain strength, call it what you will, moral strength or other strength; let us use it properly . . . so that we may influence those who have the power of war and peace in their hands. . . .

Such has been the international effort of many of the former colonies, now new states of Africa and Asia. Unfortunately, they have not really succeeded much better among themselves than have the great states in reducing tension and assuring peace. If inter-Arab rivalry, with Egypt opposed to Saudi Arabia and Syria opposed to Jordan, has been temporarily put aside, this has only resulted because of the 1967 Arab-Israeli conflict. North Vietnam and South Vietnam are engaged in a bitter and exhausting struggle. Pakistan and India have angrily faced each other for years over Kashmir, and India and Red China have already clashed in border disputes. The list of new frictions and new international competitions is a long and dismal one. The scale of the activity may be smaller, but the nature of the politics involved is an old and excerbating one.

National freedom has not assured peace any more than it has assured prosperity, but this discouraging observation should not lead to unrelieved gloom. At least the right of peoples to determine their own destinies has been granted; the age of colonial empire is finished.

The nations of the world face their problems jointly and more equally than ever before. What happens in Jackson, Mississippi; Sharpeville, South Africa; Budapest, Hungary; or Peking, China, is no longer far away or exotic, but near and relevant. If the nations of the Third World must face their own problems, these problems are also the world's to help solve.

In this age of rich nations and poor nations, crowded on a globe in which any one point of the compass is but a few hours away at most from any other point, humanitarian concerns must override national ones. This is a thought which has provided the theme for many books, lectures, and speeches by a wide variety of economists, political scientists, and statesmen. But it has lost none of its poignancy or relevancy in the retelling.

The rich nations, notably the United States, are in a position to help the Third World realize some of its objectives, to effect the social and economic revolution of which it has dreamed. More generous foreign aid and more unqualified foreign aid must be given. More consideration must be given to world prices and their regulation so that no one nation is placed at a particular disadvantage. As the Secretary-General of the United Nations, U Thant, said recently:

We must act with more authority on the world's economic problems. I would like all foreign-aid programs to operate multilaterally through the U.N. And we must attack the economic injustice that leaves so many needy nations hopelessly dependent on world prices for their primary commodities. There can be no whole world at peace—with half the world in want.

As long as the world remains so unequally divided and as long as the superpowers seek political advantages in the former colonial territories, accusations of imperialism and neo-colonialism will continue to be made. Indeed, with Communist China's pretension to world power, the cries have not lessened but have increased. Even the Soviet Union is condemned by its erstwhile ally of collusion with the imperialists of the West. Yet, for better and for worse, most of the peoples of the contemporary world are governed by their own representatives. In the Third World democracy may not be a flourishing institution and republicanism may often mean nothing more than dictatorship or one-party rule, but one can only hope that such situations are transitory, the time of troubles accompanying any revolutionary period.

Whatever the situation, it is to the rich nations and the former colonial powers to give inspiration rather than to read moral lessons. Or put otherwise, their task is to fulfill generously the international responsibility nobly formulated by the colonial theorists of a half-century ago and not yet realized.

7 . EUROPEAN IMPERIALISM IN RETROSPECT

Empire was once a word which inspired confidence, aroused enthusiasm, and suggested a glory that was not ephemeral. Today it is no longer an evocative word employed by politicians and public orators to swell the pride of their listeners. The few remaining empires in name— and none is colonial—are not awesome and suggest no threat to international peace and no strong disposition to expansion.

Whether imperialism can therefore be considered a force of the past is a moot question. The Soviet Union and Communist China have engaged in political practices within the last two decades which are imperialistic in all but name. And several new nations in Africa and Asia covet their neighbor's territory with much of the earnestness and self-righteousness mustered by European proponents of imperialism only a few dozen years ago.

The history of imperialism perhaps will never be fully written as long as greed, envy, and lust for power are harbored by men and the governments they compose. But that subject is more the concern of the psychologist and philosopher than of the historian.

As for European overseas empire, however, there is no doubt as to its finality. For four hundred years it arched majestically yet threateningly over world affairs, but it has now disintegrated. Perhaps Europe is the weaker as the result, but the world at large is the stronger for it. Yet while it will do little good to moralize about this particular imperialist phenomenon, there is value in offering a final assessment of its significance.

If one were to assign the purposes of imperialism to one academic category, it would be to the political one. Although its economic and social effects were the most significant, empire was from the European perspective essentially a political undertaking and one that was most easily explained in terms of power politics. But, interestingly enough, imperialism was seldom at the heart of European concerns. As Dehio suggested in his *Precarious Balance*, empires were on the flanks, and if they were weights and counterweights in the European balance of power, they were hardly ever considered indispensable. Always empire was seen as an additional, not the major, source of a nation's strength. Throughout its history as the world's dominant power complex, Europe turned in on itself even when it turned out to annex the world.

Yet empire was never incidental. Voltaire might cynically have commented in *Candide* that Canada was but a few acres of snow, and early-nineteenth-century English personalities might have publicly declaimed that colonies were more of a burden than a boon, but imperialist activities and relationships were always carefully added into any political reckoning. What empire really did politically was extend the European political system into a world political system, joining the many parts of the world together and entangling them in the complicated skein of political ties between Berlin, London, Paris, Rome, The Hague, and Madrid.

Perhaps this historical observation helps one in appreciating the relative ease with which imperial devolution took place. The stakes were seldom high enough for a nation to jeopardize its well-being and its existence on this or that segment of empire. Soon after General de Gaulle came to power, even the French gave up their obstinate insistence that "Algérie, c'est la France." The drain of the Algerian war on the nation's economy had been great, and the existence of the state was seriously threatened by it. Indeed, the weak Fourth Republic toppled as a result.

Of course one can insist that empire collapsed because the Europeans no longer had the strength or the will to fight to hold it, because they were moved by democratic and liberal principles which were now seriously bothering their consciences. Yet these considerations do not detract from the fact that empires were not really central to European power.

Much the same argument can be made about the economic value of empire. Trade and investment statistics reveal the same peripheral relationship of colonial produce and markets to European and American ones. Ironically, perhaps, the great age of European-African trade is the one that began as empire disintegrated.

None of the foregoing, however, admits of the conclusion that European imperialism was insignificant in terms of European affairs. The friction over Fashoda in 1898 or over the two Moroccan crises at the beginning of the twentieth century surely indicate that the value of empire was never debased. As was suggested at the beginning of this study, overseas empire was seen as a means of enhancing the economic and political strength of the European nations. And if one considers the military support the dominions provided England both in the Boer War and World War I, or the number of West Africans who fought on the side of France for a cause that certainly was not their own in 1914, the political value of empire is readily seized.

The perplexing question which has to be answered is this: was empire of greater significance to the Europeans or to the peoples who fell under it? Certainly, there was no one-way traffic in ideas, goods, techniques, and values. The fascination with *chinoiserie* in eighteenth-century Europe, the influence of Confucianism on French Enlightenment thought, the importance of tobacco, coffee, potatoes, and cocoa on the eating and social habits of Europeans, all indicate that the Third World had its stimulating effects on the West. But the total list that can be drawn up cannot match in significance the European one. For, quite simply, the effects of Europe on the Third World were revolutionary, while the effects of the Third World on Europe were not. We now return, of necessity, to the question of modernization.

While it might do for antiquarians and sentimentalists to lament the passing of the old society, and while contemporary African politicians may invoke the values of communal, tribal Africa as meaningful for the 1960's, no one who tries to view the matter with some detachment can escape the conclusion that the economic and social evolution of the contemporary world is proceeding along a one-way road of no return. And this leads to the rationalized, industrial, urban society which Europe first achieved and to which she introduced the rest of the world. It is this society, and no other, which has enabled man to satisfy his wants, fulfill his aspirations, and achieve a certain degree of equality undreamed of this side of heaven by preceding generations.

It is easy to err on the side of generosity to the Europeans when making such an assessment. As has already been emphasized several times, the results achieved were more often accidental and unintentional than gloriously calculated. Arnold Toynbee has amassed an impressive array of metaphors to describe the process, from cultural rays to cultural splinters. What he is trying to suggest is the disruptive influence which the new European ideas and techniques had on the old order. A missionary here, a hospital there, a military outpost somewhere else, and a new urban complex everywhere were intrusions which could not be easily accounted for in traditional terms and which, more significantly, stood as indications of the dynamic qualities and the relative superiority of this foreign culture over the local one.

Further qualification is necessary. The relativity of values—of Christianity against Buddhism, of Confucius against Plato, or of the Benin bronzes against the Ghiberti bronze doors in Florence—is gainsaid. Only the snob or the boor would try to arrange them all on a nicely incremented scale. But the value of Europe's material culture was not relative; it was absolute. And it almost forced the acceptance of the idea of the superiority of the rest of the European cultural baggage. There was a daemonic quality about the steam engine, the telegraph, the machine gun, which suggested a spiritual as well as a technological superiority. One remembers the vivid account in Conrad's *Heart of Darkness* of the African fireman's concern and respect for the small steam engine which he tended on the river boat wending its way up the Congo. And the famous Cargo Cult of the Pacific islands also suggests the awe and concern which were frequently expressed over European techniques and ways.

Let us be bold and say that for better rather than for worse the indigenous populations began to accept, to imitate the European ways and to discard their old traditions or to modify them in accordance with the newfound truths and techniques.

Yet what Africans and Asians were doing was following a pattern less than two centuries old in Europe. The nineteenth-century peasant who worked the lands of France or who served his master as serf in Russia followed the time-worn and inefficient methods that had been bequeathed by his father before him. When the steam engine first cut across the meadows of Europe, it aroused the wrath of the Romantics, who saw here the desecration of their sylvan world; it frightened the cottagers, who saw it as a monster belching fire and steam; and it invoked the religious scourge of those who saw it as a corrupting influence—particularly when it ran on pleasure excursions on Sunday. Moreover, need one recall the opposition to Pasteur's system of inoculation or the belief in spontaneous generation prevalent in that Europe which was already imperialistically inclined? In short, Europe's leap into the future was but a brief moment ahead of the rest of the world's. That it was successfully accomplished and the Third World's still is not has nothing to do with differences between the peoples concerned.

The danger in assessing European material superiority is in attributing it to a complex of innate European traits. Assessed in global and historical terms, the European supremacy derived first from geographical advantages: location of natural resources, well-knit fluvial systems, good harbors, fertile fields, a climate more benign than pernicious. But even more it results from a coincidence of historical and cultural factors, of the interplay of other civilizations and foreign ideas on the people of the West: of Hellenic, Roman, and Byzantine elements, of Judaism and Christianity, of barbarian invasions from Hun and Tartar.

Quite possibly western civilization incorporated into its structure a wider variety of incompatible elements than did any other civilization of the world; and the prolonged and endless growth of the West, repeatedly rejecting its now potentially "classical" formulations, may have related to the contrarities built into its structure. No other civilized society has ever approached such restless instability. . . .[1]

The dynamism of the West, of which technological innovation is perhaps the most striking characteristic, stood in sharp contrast to the staticism of other cultures. What Nehru said of the British in India in his *Discovery of India* has almost universal application throughout the Third World:

The impact of Western culture on India was the impact of a dynamic society, of a "modern" consciousness, on a static society wedded to medieval habits of thought, which, however sophisticated and advanced in its own way, could not progress because of its inherent limitations.

The qualities of the West, then, were disruptive, and however restricted they might have been geographically in the colonial regions, they were nonetheless profoundly significant. The urban complexes of New Delhi, Hong Kong, Casablanca, Johannesburg, or Leopoldville had

[1] William McNeill, *The Rise of the West* (New York, 1965), p. 593.

an attraction which reached out to the bush and the jungle, pulling peoples away from the old and toward the new. And so did the railroad, Christianity, regularized taxation, military and labor service work their effects over wide tracts of land and among diverse populations.

If it was a small elite who were first made familiar with Western ideas and techniques and who comprehended with a critical faculty what European imperialism did and could mean, the ultimate significance of the European presence was no smaller because of this. Arnold Toynbee has said somewhere in his lengthy study of civilization that it is a cultural elite which inspires and leads the masses. Such a sociological notion may be offensive to democratic sensibilities, but this does not affect its meaning. The process of modernization taking place in the Third World today is a process which is rather pyramidal in form; an apex of leadership ruling over a large and still unformed mass at the base. And this apex still is chiefly made up of European-trained lawyers, philosophers, engineers, and schoolteachers. Thus has European influence extended, first narrowly and then broadly, so that today the notion of modernity varies but slightly between France and Senegal, Britain and India, whatever variations in political systems may separate them.

The inescapable and the chief conclusion to be drawn is the obvious one: European overseas imperialism was a cultural force of a magnitude and speed which has never been matched in history. Cultural diffusion which had extended over centuries before had led to an evolutionary absorption, but that of late nineteenth-century imperialism extended only over decades and led to revolutionary situations.

Historically, then, European overseas imperialism is one of the most significant occurrences in the modern era. The only other series of events which can possibly match it were the political and economic revolutions which shook Europe in the eighteenth and nineteenth centuries. As they changed the European political and social order, so has imperialism changed the order of the Third World.

If the perspective is broadened to include the whole range of recorded history, European overseas imperialism still stands out boldly. Only Roman, Chinese, and, perhaps, Arab imperialism before it, had such significant and long-range effects, providing new ideas and institutions which left a permanent impact on the societies affected: the Mediterranean and much of Western Europe, for the first one; Southeast Asia and Japan, for the second; the Middle East and North Africa, for the third. But the dimensions of European empire exceeded those of the preceding three. Whether the positive cultural effects will prove to be more profound, however, only the passing of centuries will tell. Yet as a disruptive influence, European imperialism occupies a unique position in world history.

By the sea the Europeans came, and by the sea they have now left. The maritime era closes with the imperialist one. The world is now of different proportions, so that the old mercator map with Europe placed at the center of a flattened globe is badly out of shape, as it is out of date.

What a vain and pretentious attitude and yet what an audacious and dedicated one that caused men to venture out on uncharted seas to lands unknown and to assume that they had the duty and the authority to make other peoples do their bidding. It all forms a romantic and a tragic history—and a vivid introduction to our contemporary world.

FOR FURTHER READING

Any subject as immense in scope and as extended in time as European imperialism is bound to be surrounded by a rich and varied bibliography. The editions listed are those which are most readily available. It is designed to accommodate the reader who wishes to explore further but who is in need of general directions. (The following bibliographical appraisal is highly selective of the quantities of studies available in English.)

THEORIES OF IMPERIALISM

A sub-literature seems to have grown out of this subject, with the two classics remaining: J. A. Hobson, *Imperialism a Study* (London: George Allen and Unwin, 1954), and V. I. Lenin, *Imperialism the Highest Stage of Capitalism* (New York: International Publishers, 1939). The often prescribed antidote to these economic interpretations is Joseph Schumpeter's "Sociology

of Imperialism," available in an American version, edited by
P. M. Sweezy, *Imperialism and Social Classes* (New York:
Meridian, 1951). One of the earlier and successful appraisals of
the significant theoretical literature is E. M. Winslow, *The Pattern of Imperialism: A Study in Theories of Power* (New York:
Columbia University Press, 1948). A more recent analysis of
contemporary studies is D. K. Fieldhouse, "'Imperialism': A
Historiographical Revision," *The Economic History Review*, XIV,
No. 2 (1961), 187–209. David Healy has done a masterful job
of synthesizing the important works in English in *Modern Imperialism: Changing Styles in Historical Interpretation* (Washington: American Historical Association, 1967).

GENERAL STUDIES

Most general approaches to European imperialism have been less
than all-encompassing, with definition restricted by epoch or
phase, or with definition following the contours of colonial nation
or overseas region. For the first phase, or "wave" of imperialism
—that covering the fifteenth through the eighteenth centuries—
the best introduction is the brief but incisive study of J. H. Parry,
The Establishment of European Hegemony, 1415–1715 (New
York: Harper, 1961). The same author has provided a longer
and graceful study, *The Age of Reconnaissance* (Cleveland:
World, 1963), which appears to be a valuable extension and
enrichment of his earlier work. The reader in search of a brief
introduction might also consult Charles Nowell, *The Great Dis-
coveries and the First Colonial Empires* (Ithaca: Cornell University Press, 1953).

The new "wave" of imperialism, which broke in the late
nineteenth century, has launched a large number of books.
D. K. Fieldhouse, *Colonial Empires Since the Eighteenth Century* (New York: Dell, 1967) is an important and well-defined
general history. Still commendable, although old and unrevised,
is Parker T. Moon, *Imperialism and World Politics* (New York:
Macmillan, 1941). Mary E. Townsend, *European Colonial Expansion since 1871* (Philadelphia: Lippincott, 1941) is the least
interesting of the three studies here mentioned. William A.
Langer, *Diplomacy of Imperialism, 1890–1902* (New York:
Knopf, 1935; 2 vols.) has the justly-earned status of a classic.

On the national level Great Britain has received the most extensive historical treatment. A very readable, albeit at times sen-
timental, study is Charles E. Carrington, *The British Overseas:*

Exploits of a Nation of Shopkeepers (Cambridge: Cambridge University Press, 1951). Institutions and policies are well combined in Eric A. Walker, *The British Empire, Its Structure and Spirit, 1497–1953* (Cambridge, Mass.: Harvard University Press, 1956). Of the majestical *Cambridge History of the British Empire*, Volume III: *The Empire-Commonwealth, 1870–1919* (Cambridge: Cambridge University Press, 1959) merits special citation.

Unfortunately, there is still no outstanding, comprehensive history in English on the French colonial empire. Still useful are Herbert I. Priestley, *France Overseas through the Old Regime* (New York: Appleton-Century, 1939), and the same author's, *France Overseas: A Study of Modern Imperialism* (New York: Appleton-Century, 1938.) Similarly dated but useful is Stephen Roberts, *A History of French Colonial Policy, 1870–1925* (London: King and Son, 1929; 2 vols.). The most interesting recent work, and now available in English, is Henri Brunschwig, *French Colonialism, 1871–1914: Myths and Realities* (New York: Praeger, 1966). Its forceful revisionist thesis, which places great emphasis on nationalism, is worth attention.

German colonial history fares little better than French insofar as a good, general study in English is concerned. One might still turn with profit to Mary E. Townsend, *The Origins of Modern German Colonialism* (New York: Columbia University Press, 1921), or her *The Rise and Fall of the German Colonial Empire, 1884–1918* (New York: Macmillan, 1930). A. J. P. Taylor has offered a well-argued interpretation which suggests that Germany's colonial efforts were subordinate to, indeed used to enhance, Germany's European diplomatic position: *Germany's First Bid for Colonies, 1884–1885* (London: Macmillan, 1938). Of the several recent works dealing with aspects of German expansionism, the anthology edited by Prosser Gifford and Wm. Roger Louis, *Britain and Germany in Africa* (New Haven: Yale University Press, 1967) is outstanding, both in the quality of analysis and the range of material. This same volume should be consulted for the British role in Africa.

Concerning the older and lesser colonial empires there are several good introductory studies. Two appear in a well-ordered series edited by J. H. Plumb, *The History of Human Society*. They are: J. H. Parry, *The Spanish Seaborne Empire* (New York: Knopf, 1966); and C. R. Boxer, *The Dutch Seaborne Empire, 1600–1800* (New York: Knopf, 1965). Also the reader might consult James Duffy, *Portugal in Africa* (Cambridge,

Mass.: Harvard University Press, 1962); C. R. Boxer's brief, but suggestive study, *Four Centuries of Portuguese Expansion, 1415–1825* (Johannesburg: University of Witwatersrand Press, 1961); and Ruth Slade's straight-forward history, *King Leopold's Congo* (New York: Oxford University Press, 1962).

COLONIAL DEVOLUTION AND INDEPENDENCE

This subject has been the vital center of some of the most exciting and valuable academic debate in recent years. Theories of modernization, of revolution, and of international politics here converge and, often, confuse. By far the best introductory work is Rupert Emerson, *From Empire to Nation* (Boston: Beacon Press, 1962). Of importance are: Gabriel Almond and James Coleman, *The Politics of Developing Areas* (Princeton: Princeton University Press, 1960); Fatma Mansur, *The Process of Independence* (London: Routledge and Kegan Paul, 1963). On the theory of modernization two studies merit attention as pacesetters: Daniel Lerner, *The Passing of Traditional Society* (Glencoe: The Free Press, 1958), which centers on the Middle East; and Lucien Pye, *Politics, Personality and Nation Building* (New Haven: Yale University Press, 1961), which is concerned with Burma. On economic aspects of the problem of post-colonial development Gunnar Myrdal, *Economic Theory and the Under-Developed Regions* (London: Duckworth, 1957); and Albert O. Hirshman, *The Strategy of Economic Development* (New Haven: Yale University Press, 1965) provide stimulating interpretations. Eugene Staley, *The Future of Underdeveloped Countries* (New York: Praeger, 1961) thoughtfully covers both economic and political problems.

PERSONAL PERSPECTIVES

Some of the most interesting and revealing literature concerning the process and effects of imperialism is that provided by people whose lives were directly affected by the occurrence. Highly commended is Jawaharlal Nehru, *Toward Freedom* (New York: John Day, 1942), the autobiography of the great Indian leader. Albert Schweitzer, *On the Edge of the Primeval Forest* (New York: Macmillan, 1948) offers vivid description of and sincere reflection on this world famous humanitarian's first encounter with Equatorial Africa. Isak Dinesen, *Out of Africa* (New York: Modern Library, 1952) skillfully captures a particular mood of life on a Kenyan plantation between the two world wars. Among the many novels in which the effects of the colonial presence on local life is a significant theme, E. M. Forster, *A Passage to India* (New York: Harcourt, Brace and World, 1952) and Chinua Achebe, *Things Fall Apart* (New York: Honor Books, 1959) are particularly suggestive and sensitive.

INDEX

DATE DUE

MAR 30 '70			
NOV 20 '73			
DEC 11 '73			
GAYLORD			PRINTED IN U.S.A.